WBDP The West Bank Data Base Project

1987 REPORT

Demographic, economic, legal, social and political developments in the West Bank

Meron Benvenisti

THE JERUSALEM POST

Routledge
Taylor & Francis Group
LONDON AND NEW YORK

First published 1987 by Westview Press

Published 2019 by Routledge
52 Vanderbilt Avenue, New York, NY 10017
2 Park Square, Milton Park, Abingdon, Oxon OX14 4RN

Routledge is an imprint of the Taylor & Francis Group, an informa business

ISBN 13: 978-0-367-27372-9 (hbk)
ISBN 13: 978-0-367-27410-8 (pbk)

INTRODUCTION

The present survey is the fourth compiled by the West Bank Data Base Project, during its five years of operation. The first report was published in September 1982 (Interim Report No.1, West Bank Data Base Project, Jerusalem, 1982); the second in April 1984 (West Bank Data Base Project: A Survey of Israel's Policies, American Enterprise Institute, Washington D.C., 1984); the third, in February 1986 (1986 Report, West Bank Data Base Project and the Jerusalem Post, Jerusalem, 1986).

The 1987 survey deals with developments in the territories during 1986 and early 1987. We have dispensed with footnotes and references in the text. A list of sources used in the Report is appended. We draw heavily upon the retrieval system of the West Bank Data Base Project located in Jerusalem, which is in the public domain.

Section one was compiled by the Project's research team, Section two was written, in part, by Dr. Simcha Bahiri. Research for Section four was done by Susan Podziba. Word processing was done by Hannah Orgel. The report was edited by Polly Amkraut. As in previous reports, the concluding section is written in the form of a conceptual essay.

The undersigned takes full responsibility for all value judgments, opinions and errors.

Meron Benvenisti

Jerusalem, August 1987

LIST OF MAPS AND CHARTS

Sources:

Figures 1,2,3,4,5 – from: Dehter, A., How Expensive Are West Bank Settlements, West Bank Data Base Project and the Jerusalem Post, 1987.

Figures 6,7,8,9 – from: Khayat S., Turner M., Benvenisti M., The West Bank: A Generation After, West Bank Data Base Project and the Jerusalem Post, Forthcoming.

TABLE OF CONTENTS

LIST OF TABLES

ONE: DEMOGRAPHIC TRENDS

By the end of 1985, the latest end of year for which official data are available, the Palestinian population of the occupied territories reached 1,339,000 inhabitants, 813,000 in the West Bank (excluding 125,000 in East Jerusalem), and 525,000 in the Gaza Strip (for Israeli population in the territories, see below, section five). Based on the growth rates of 1984-1985, the total population figures for the end of 1986 have reached 1,377,000 (835,000 in the West Bank and 542,000 in Gaza). The 1986 figures represent an increase of 40 percent since September 1967 (when the first and only census was taken in the area by the Israelis), and 45 percent more than in 1970 (when war related migrations came to an end).

Annual population increase in 1984-1986 has been slightly less than 3 percent in the West Bank and slightly more than 3 percent in the Gaza Strip. This rate of increase, one of the highest attained during Israeli occupation, stems from the same demographic trends detected since 1983. These are: reduction of net migration, sustained natality rates and somewhat reduced mortality rates. Annual live births in the territories reached 57,000 in 1985-1986, and net migration during the same years was 10,000 persons per annum (compared to 17-18,000 in the mid 1970's). Crude birth rates (revised estimates) in 1986 were over 42 per thousand in the West Bank, and over 45 per thousand in Gaza. Total fertility rates were around 7 births per woman (revised data). These were similar to those prevailing in the past 6-7 years, and 40 percent higher than those recorded among Israeli Muslims. The only long-term significant change in fertility patterns since 1981 is a shift in the peak fertility age from 25-29 to 30-31, probably caused by postponed marriages. Past high fertility and reduced net migration contributed to the rapid population growth in the parental ages, hence the increase in absolute annual number of births. Sustained fertility and decreased migration create the preconditions for sustained high natality rates in the next two decades, even if fertility rates are about to decline (see below).

During the early 1980s, almost one third of the women in the 20-39 age group gave birth annually. This is only a slightly smaller percentage than that of 15 years earlier, and significantly higher than that prevailing among the Israeli Muslims (22 percent). Moreover, the fertility of women in the 20-39 age group contributed almost 90 percent to the total fertility rate among Israeli Muslims, but only 83 percent among the women in the territories. These ratios indicate that in the territories, childbearing is still almost evenly distributed during a long life span and that fertility control has not really spread out. The only fairly visible sign of some fertility limitation can be found at the very old ages beyond 45. This group averages 23-28 births per thousand women which is 3 to 4 times higher than the prevailing rate in Israeli Muslim women of the same age group.

According to official sources, mortality is poorly recorded. Under-registration is believed to be particularly high for infants and children. Recorded infant mortality rates are less than 30 per thousand in the West Bank and less than 40 per thousand in the Gaza Strip. The CBS assesses those rates at about 60 per thousand in the mid 1980's. According to the Ministry of Health data, high rates of recorded infant mortality are due to infectious and other ecologically related diseases, which indirectly strengthen the CBS assessment of considerably higher infant mortality incidence than that recorded.

In the long range, however, infant mortality rates have decreased from about 150 per thousand live births of the early and late sixties (data drawn from the 1961 Jordanian census and the 1967 Israeli census) to the present levels. Two main reasons might have contributed to such a decline:

a) The percentage of birth occurring in clinical facilities (hospitals, medical centres, etc.) has continuously increased since 1968 and reached in 1985 55 percent in the West bank and 57 percent in the Gaza Strip, which is more than a four-fold increase in 18 years.
b) The expanding vaccination network in the West Bank and the Gaza Strip which presently covers almost all children of vaccination age.

Population Distribution

All the current trends of the Palestinian population in the occupied territories are conducive to "young" age structures. The relatively large migration of the mid and late 1970's mainly drained young people of pre-parental or early parental ages (15-29). Hence, from 1967 to the very early 1980's, the percentage of children under the age of 15 gradually diminished. Since 1982 this percentage has either maintained its level (46.4 -46.6 percent in the West Bank) or slightly increased it (from 47.4 in 1982 to 47.8 in 1984 in the Gaza Strip). Some age groups have been particularly depleted by the emigration during the occupation period.

The following approximate calculations (Table 1) have been made by comparing the size of an age group at the end of 1967 with an estimated size of the age group 20 years later, in 1987. Almost all of the differences may be attributed to emigration, since the selected age groups were young enough that mortality can therefore be disregarded.

TABLE 1
SELECTED AGE GROUPS DEPLETED BY EMIGRATION
1967 – 1987

Age in 1967	Persons in 1967	% remained in 1987(a)	Age in 1987
West Bank			
10-14	80,500	60	30-34
15-19	50,000	45	35-39
20-24	36,700	57	40-44
Gaza Strip			
10-14	55,600	65	30-34
15-19	37,800	53	35-39
20-24	25,000	56	40-44

Of the three selected age groups, those who were in their late teens in 1967 participated in the migration outflows to the largest extent. At least one out of two in the West Bank, and almost as many as that in the Gaza Strip have left the area. This is explained by their being the optimum ages (early to mid-twenties) for migrant labor in the mid-seventies, when oil production expanded rapidly and caused an economic boom in Arab oil producing countries.

In addition, about 40 percent of the younger and older generations were depleted by emigration. An obvious consequence of the depletion trend of the groups aged 10-24 in

1967, and that of the increase in absolute numbers of births during the 1970's is, that by the mid 1980's the absolute and relative share of the population under the age of 35 rose more than average. The reason is that they belong to age groups far more numerous than the older ones. They were either too young in 1967 to be seriously affected by the emigration, or came of age during lower emigration periods in the eighties. For example, the current number of persons aged 25-34 in the West Bank doubled in a decade, while the number of those aged 35-49 has slightly decreased. The implications of this trend on school and college development, on the labor force and job creation policy are far reaching, but exceed the scope of this report.

Projections

The CBS has recently published official population projections until 2002 for the West Bank and the Gaza Strip. Apparently this is the first time that such official demographic forecasts have been published. The main variable component concerns migration-balance during the projected period. Three alternative assumptions have been introduced.

1. Zero annual migration balance (i.e. no emigration)
2. Negative annual migration balance, equal to the rate in recent years, i.e. 8.0 per thousand for the West Bank and 6.5 per thousand for the Gaza Strip.
3. Negative annual migration of 10.0 per thousand for both areas.

TABLE 2
PROJECTIONS TO 2002 OF THE POPULATIONS
IN THE WEST BANK AND GAZA STRIP (BASE: 1985)
(thousand)

	Gaza Strip	West Bank	Total
End of 1985	526	813	1,339
Projections to 2002			
Projection 1	992	1,429	2,421
Projection 2	865	1,221	2,076
Projection 3	789	1,136	1,925

Total fertility rates will diminish to 5 births per woman in the West Bank and 5.7 births in the Gaza Strip. Mortality will decrease, and life expectancy will rise from 63 to 69 years by the end of the century.

The share of children under 15 will decrease in 2002. Total number of children will increase by 40 percent and will reach 860,000 – 1 million. Dependency ratios will decrease and the growth of persons in their prime would be higher than the growth of the general population. An increase in the population of women in the fertility ages (15-49) (approximately 20 percent higher than the general population growth) will increase absolute birth figures, despite the projected decrease in fertility rates.

Official CBS population projections confirm WBDP forecasts published in our 1986 report, which stated (p.4) that "by the year 2000 West Bank and Gaza population together would approach two million". Also, the share of the Jewish population in the areas of Mandatory Palestine will decrease from 63 percent in 1984 to 61 percent in 1990, and 55 percent to 57 percent by 2000. West Bank and Gaza population would constitute 28 percent of the total Mandatory Palestine population (compared to 24 percent in 1985), and Israeli Arabs (including East Jerusalem) 15-17 percent. All other things being equal, by the year 2010 Jewish and Arab populations will attain parity.

TWO: ECONOMIC DEVELOPMENTS

Gross Domestic Product (GDP)

The domestic economy of the West Bank and Gaza Strip represent a fraction of Israel's GDP (at official figures less than 4.5 percent). Despite its small size, statistics are notoriously conflicting and often inaccurate. Nevertheless, they do serve as an indicator of major developments and trends. It is important to note, however, that the GDP (1980-1985) represents only some two thirds (68 percent) of the Gross National Disposable Income (GNDI)which is equal to the GDP+net factor payments from abroad(GNP)+net current transfers from abroad. At market values the GDP of the territories equals some $1 billion as compared to $1.5 billion for the GNDI – one of the highest differentials in the world.

Table 3 is a comparative analysis of the 1985 GDP of the West Bank and Gaza Strip with Israel. As the GDP of the West Bank/Gaza Strip is in factor prices, the data is understated by around 5 percent. Only agriculture represents a significant fraction of Israel's magnitude (nearly 20 percent). In employment it was 40 percent.

The low level of productivity (GDP per worker) as compared to Israel is noteworthy. It is about 40 percent of GDP per worker in Israel (in general) and less than 20 percent of GDP per worker in industry. Industry is the most backward sector of the economy. Construction is the most productive – nearly 60 percent of Israel's GDP per worker, which is in itself low due to cheap (Arab) labor preventing the introduction of more modern technology.

The same data source (see Table 4) shows a comparison over time of the GDP in 1980 prices, e.g. the annual growth rates between 1980 and 1985. The GDP only grew at the nominal annual rate of 0.4 percent between 1980 and 1983, with an annual average population increase of over 2.5 percent. This represents a 2 percent

TABLE 3

1985 GDP, EMPLOYMENT AND PRODUCTIVITY IN ISRAEL, WEST BANK AND GAZA STRIP*

	Israel		West Bank		Gaza Strip		Wb/GS		WB/GS as % of Israel
	$ mill.	%	$ mill.	%	$ mill.	%	$ mill.	%	
Gross Domestic Product**	22,050	100	694	100	249	100	943	100	4.3
Agriculture	1,323	6	209	30.2	44	17.8	253	26.9	19.1
Industry	5,513	25	55	7.9	22	8.7	77	8.1	1.4
Construction	1,764	8	110	15.8	44	17.8	154	16.4	8.7
Services	13,450	61	320	46.1	139	55.7	459	48.6	3.4
	Thous.	%	Thous.	%	Thous.	%	Thous.	%	%
Employed	1,457***	100	103.7	100	48.9	100	152.6	100	10.5
Agriculture	92	6.3	28.4	27.4	8.8	18	37.2	24.3	40.4
Industry	332	22.8	16.7	16.1	7.9	16.2	24.6	16.1	7.4
Construction	115	7.9	12.8	12.3	4.1	8.4	16.9	11.1	14.7
Services	918	63	45.8	44.2	28.2	57.4	73.9	48.5	8.1
	$	%	$	%	$	%	$	%	%
GDP/Employment	15,130	100	6,690	100	5,090	100	6,180	100	40.8
Agriculture	14,380	95	7,360	110	5,000	98	6,800	110	47.3
Industry	16,600	110	3,290	49	2,780	55	3,130	51	18.9
Construction	15,340	101	8,590	128	10,730	211	9,110	147	59.4
Services	14,150	97	6,990	104	4,930	97	6,210	101	42.4

* Source: Statistical Abstract of Israel, 1986 and Administrative Territories Quarterly, December 1986.

** At factor costs for the West Bank and Gaza Strip and for Israel in market prices. Both at exchange rate of NIS 1.179 = $1. The GDP at market prices for the WB is $734 million and for the GS $263 million for a total of $997 million.

*** Includes 89,000 workers from WB/GS.

per capita annual drop in GDP over the period. In absolute terms there was a 4.2 percent drop in the value of agricultural product over the half decade which is nearly 7 percent per capita drop. Even industry and construction grew less than the population. Only the service sector showed a real increase.

One of the factors influencing economic developments in the West Bank/Gaza Strip is the pervasive impact of the Israeli economy. The Israeli GDP between 1980 and 1985 grew at an average rate of 2.2 percent or less than 1/2 percent per capita. The GNP per capita remained stagnant over this period.

However, there were significant differences in development between the economies of the West Bank and the Gaza Strip. The biggest drop in agriculture occurred in the West Bank where despite the low olive crop in 1985, industry (including olive oil) increased by 2.8 percent as against a drop of 1.1 percent in the Gaza Strip. This reverses the trend in the 1970's when the Gaza Strip was developing its industry at a faster rate than the West Bank and the GDP rose rapidly. The drop in the share of West Bank agriculture in the GDP from a third to only a quarter continues a multi-annual trend. Industry remained at under 8 percent while the large increase occurred in the (non-productive) services sector to over half of the West Bank GDP.

Developments in 1986

There has been a substantial improvement in the economy of the West Bank and Gaza in 1986. Gross Domestic Product rose by 9 percent in the West Bank and 4 percent in Gaza. Private consumption went up 7 percent or 4 percent per capita in the West Bank, and 7 percent, 3 percent per capita, in Gaza. Public consumption rose by 8 percent in the West Bank and public capital investment by 5 percent. In Gaza, public consumption increased by 3 percent and public capital investment by 4 percent.

Total employment of residents of the West Bank/Gaza Strip (both in Israel and the territories) rose from 242.1 thousand in 1985 to 261.2 thousand in 1986, an increase of 7.9 percent. Of this increase of 19.1 thousand, 5.5 thousand were employed in Israel (new total now 94.7 thousand – an increase of 8.2 percent) and 13.6

TABLE 4

GDP OF THE WEST BANK AND GAZA: 1980-1985*
(at factor prices, in 1980 prices in thousand New Shekel)

	West Bank			Gaza Strip			West Bank + Gaza Strip				
	1980	1985	% p.a. growth	1980	1985	% p.a. growth	1980	% of 1980 GDP	1985	% of 1985 GDP	% p.a. growth
Total GDP	3,905	3,949	0.2	1,448	1,525	1	5,353	100	5,474	100	0.4
Agriculture	1,490	1,110	-4.6	273	252	-1.5	1,763	32.9	1,362	24.9	-4.2
Industry	247	283	2.8	143	135	-1.1	390	7.3	418	7.6	1.4
Construction	536	623	3.1	310	256	-2.8	792	14.8	879	16.1	2.1
Services	1,632	1,933	3.4	722	882	4.1	2,354	44	2,815	51.4	3.6

* Source: Judea, Samaria and Gaza Area Statistics – November 1986 (note discrepancies with 1985 current data figure and incomplete bases of services which include imputed housing rents).

thousand employed in the territories (an increase of 8.2 percent). This increase in total employment in all sectors indicates a significant increase in economic activity in the territories.

Olive production in 1986 rose significantly over 1985, which had an extremely bad olive harvest and olive based exports. While final figures on the crop are not yet available, exports of olive oil and pickled olives rose from $715,000 in 1985 to $24.7 million or nearly to the level of 1984 ($28.5 million). Olive output impacts both industry and agriculture.

The additional number employed in West Bank/Gaza Strip industry in 1986 was 2,600 to a total of 27,200 workers which represents an increase of 10.6 percent. Industrial output in the West Bank was 29 percent higher than in 1985, caused mainly by increase in olive oil production, but also by an increase in textile production. In Gaza, industrial output rose by 13 percent.

Trade figures show a substantial increase over 1985 (see below) – especially industrial exports to Israel and Jordan. Total industrial exports from the territories reached $318 million in 1986 which, (assuming 40 percent value added), represents $127 million in industrial GDP.

Revenues of residents from employment outside the territories rose in constant prices by 3 percent in the West Bank and 1 percent in Gaza. Net income per diem from employment in Israel increased by 10 percent over 1984.

Gross Domestic Product reached US$800 million in the West Bank and US$274 million in Gaza, or a total of US$1,074 million. GNP in 1986 was US$1,028 million in the West Bank and US$456 million in Gaza (in 1985 prices).

Trade in 1986

In 1986 (see Table 5) Israel's exports to the West Bank/Gaza Strip ($780.3 million) represented 89.4 percent of their imports (same as 1985). Exports from Israel represented 10.9 percent of their export of goods and 10.2 percent export of their industrial goods; 20.4 percent of their export of agricultural goods and 14.3 percent of their export of industrial goods excluding diamonds, and 22 percent of industrial exports (defense exports are also excluded).

Imports from the West Bank/Gaza Strip to Israel ($289.1 million) represented only 3 percent of Israel's import of goods. They represented 73.2 percent of the territories exports which is higher then the 66.1 percent of 1985. Total imports from Israel (to West Bank/Gaza) increased by 30.5 percent in 1986 over 1985. Exports to Israel increased by 62.6 percent, the bulk of which came from an increase of industrial goods exported from the West Bank/Gaza Strip. The export of Israeli goods to the West Bank/Gaza Strip is second only to the U.S. market and exceeds total export to the rest of Asia and Oceania. This high level of export (and re-export) is encouraged by the high level of protection enjoyed by Israeli goods in this "common market" with the territories rather than any real comparative advantage of Israeli goods.

The surplus of exports over imports from Israel increased in 1986 to $491.2 million as compared to $405.8 million in 1985 – up by some 21 percent (see Table 4).

Exports to Jordan ($100.6 million) increased by 17.8 percent but this represents only some 25.5 percent of the West Bank/Gaza Strip exports. The trade surplus with Jordan increased by 16.9 percent in 1986 and stood at $89.7 million. Nearly all of the improvement was due to the increase in the export of olive oil ($22.3 million) and pickled olives in 1986 as compared to a ten year low of $0.7 million in 1985 (see Table 5).

Israeli exports to the territories are unrestricted while several regional commodities may not be exported to Israel (nor for that matter to Israel's traditional overseas markets). Most Israeli imports center on labor intensive textile, clothing and leather which are profitably subcontracted and returned in partial or finished form with most of the benefits accrued by Israel. Most industrial exports are linked to Israeli production.

Israel's resources were nearly $36 billion in 1985. Those of the West Bank and Gaza Strip were $1.9 billion, or only 5.3 percent of the Israeli total. This is shown in Table 8 which gives the data in dollar terms for Israel and the territories as well as in percentage of resources. It also provides a comparison with Israel and the average annual growth rates of the various parameters between 1980 and 1985.

The total resources of Israel grew at a faster rate (2.7 percent per annum) than that of the West Bank/Gaza Strip.

Private consumption represented about 64 percent of the resources for both Israel and the territories. But the territories represented only 8.6 percent of Israel's private consumption – the highest percent of any single parameter. The rate of growth of private consumption lagged behind that of Israel (3.5 percent versus 2.5 percent) – a reversal of the situation in the 1970's.

Government consumption in the West Bank/Gaza Strip was 6.8 percent of the resources compared to 20.4 percent of the resources in Israel (less than one third). This was partly, but not solely (see below), due to Israel's huge defense expenditure. In absolute terms, government consumption amounts to only 1.7 percent of Israel's. The rate of growth in public expenditure was larger than Israel's – 1.5 versus 0.5 percent per annum (see below).

Investment in both areas declined but the decline was greater in the territories (3.5 percent, versus 1.1 percent in Israel). Investment as a percent of resources was higher in the territories (14 percent) than in Israel (11.2 percent) but as a percent of GNP they were equal at 19 percent which are both too low. "Productive" investment in the territories (machinery, transport, and other equipment) was only 14 percent of total investment as compared to 58 percent in Israel. Clearly there was little "productive" investment (including transport equipment) in the West Bank/Gaza Strip.

The trade situation of the West Bank/Gaza Strip worsened with a decline in their total exports. Imports represented nearly 39 percent of resources for the West Bank/ Gaza Strip as compared to just over 29 percent for Israel.

The GDP of the occupied areas was only 4.5 percent of Israel's (6.7 percent of the GNP). In Israel the GDP was slightly higher than the GNP in contrast to West Bank/Gaza Strip where the GDP was only 71 percent of the GNP. Israel's GDP grew at over 2.2 percent per annum in contrast to West Bank/Gaza Strip which only grew at 0.5 percent. The record for their GNP was somewhat better but still below the population increase.

With an average population for Israel (including East Jerusalem and the Golan) and the West Bank/Gaza Strip of 4.233 million and 1.32 million respectively, the GNP per capita was (1986) $4,950 for

Israel and $1,124 for the territories or, 23 percent of the Israeli level. The GDP was $5,200 for Israel and $813 for the territories or, 15.6 percent. Private consumption per capita was (1985) $3,320 for Israel, $920 for the West bank and Gaza, or, less than 28 percent. Private consumption exceeded the territories' GDP by over 20 percent.

TABLE 5

FOREIGN TRADE IN GOODS: THE WEST BANK AND GAZA STRIP* (MILLIONS, U.S.$)

	West Bank	Gaza Strip	WB + GS	Percent	% change from 1985
I. Imports: Grand Total	497.8	374.7	872.5	100.0	+30.6
From Israel – Total	436.8	343.5	780.3	89.4	+30.5
Agricultural	69.7	44.7	114.4	13.1	+30.3
Industrial	367.1	298.8	665.9	76.3	+30.5
From Jordan-Total	10.9	–	10.9	1.2	+25.3
Agricultural	0.2	–	0.2	–	-33.3
Industrial	10.7	–	10.7	1.2	+27.4
From other countries-					
Total	50.1	31.2	81.3	9.3	+32.8
Agricultural	7.1	8.5	15.6	1.8	+11.4
Industrial	43	22.7	65.7	7.5	+39.2
II. Exports: Grand Total	239.3	155.7	395	100	+46.9
To Israel-Total	156	133.1	289.1	73.2	+62.6
Agricultural	16.7	13.9	30.6	7.7	+22.4
Industrial	139.3	119.2	258.5	65.4	+69.2
To Jordan-Total	81.8	18.8	100.6	25.5	+17.8
Agricultural	23.8	18.8	42.6	10.8	-12.3
Industrial	58	–	58	14.7	+57.6
To other countries-					
Total	1.5	3.8	5.3	1.3	-77.2
Agricultural	–	3.8	3.8	1	-19.1
Industrial	1.5	–	1.5	0.3	-70
III. Surplus of Imports over					
Exports-Grand Total	258.5	219	477.5	100	+24.2
In Trade with Israel	280.8	210.4	491.2	102.9	+21
In Trade with Jordan	-70.9	-18.8	-89.7	-18.8	-16.9
In Trade with Others	48.6	27.4	76	15.9	+36.9

* Source: Judea, Samaria and Gaza Area Statistics, March, 1987.

TABLE 6

1985 NATIONAL ACCOUNTS OF ISRAEL AND THE WEST BANK/GAZA STRIP*
(in million U.S.$ at market prices at NIS 1.179 = U.S.$1)

	Israel		West Bank		Gaza Strip		WB + GS		WB/GS as % of	% p.a. Change 1980/5	% p.a. change 1980/5
	Mill. $	% of Res.	Mill. $	% of Res.	Mill. $	% of Res.	Mill. $	% of Res.	Israel	Israel	WB/GS
Resources	35,936	100.0	1,279	100.0	629	100.0	1,908	100.0	5.3	2.7	0.8
Private Consumption	14,041	39.1	823	64.3	387	61.5	1,210	63.4	8.6	3.5	2.5
Government Consumption	7,317	20.4	87	6.8	38	6.0	125	6.6	1.7	0.5	1.5
Gross Capital Formation	4,030	11.2	186	14.5	81	12.9	267	14.0	6.9	-1.1	-3.5
Exports	10,548	29.4	183	14.3	123	19.6	306	16.0	2.9	4.9	-0.3
Imports	13,912	38.7	375	29.3	366	58.2	741	38.8	5.3	3.4	1.1
Gross Domestic Product	22,024	61.3	734	57.4	263	41.8	997	52.3	4.5	2.2	0.5
Net Factor Payments	-1,075	-3.0	218	17.0	189	30.0	407	21.3	–	-9.0	2.6
Gross National Product	20,948	58.3	952	74.4	452	71.9	1,404	73.6	6.7	1.9	1.1

* Source: Israel-Statistical Abstract of Israel, 1986
WB & GS – Judea, Samaria and Gaza Area Statistics, November, 1986.

TABLE 7

WB/GS IMPORTS, EXPORTS AND FOREIGN TRADE

		Trade with other countries			Trade with Jordan			Trade with Israel			Total		
		Balance	Exports	Imports	Balance	Exports	Imports	Balance	Exports	Imports	Balance	Exports	Imports
Judea and Samaria	1969	-5.1	0.4	5.5	11.3	18.4	7.1	-39.0	12.3	51.3	-32.8	31.1	63.9
	1970	-6.2	0.4	6.6	10.2	13.8	3.6	-38.4	16.3	54.7	-34.4	30.5	64.9
	1971	-11.0	0.5	11.5	15.0	18.8	3.8	-39.6	20.9	60.5	-35.6	40.2	75.8
	1972	-12.3	0.4	12.7	21.0	25.5	4.5	-55.6	25.6	81.2	-46.9	51.5	98.4
	1973	-9.7	0.4	10.1	11.9	15.8	3.9	-76.7	41.6	118.3	-74.5	57.8	132.3
	1974	-14.6	0.7	15.3	21.4	26.2	4.8	-109.2	62.8	172.0	-102.4	89.7	192.1
	1975	-16.7	4.4	21.1	29.7	34.7	5.0	-134.1	69.9	204.0	-121.1	109.0	230.1
	1976	-18.5	3.5	22.0	38.9	42.6	3.7	-145.0	77.1	222.1	-124.6	123.2	247.8
	1977	-21.2	1.0	22.2	39.1	43.8	4.7	-166.0	73.6	239.6	-148.1	118.4	266.5
	1978	-27.5	1.3	28.8	56.6	61.6	5.0	-139.2	77.9	217.1	-110.1	140.8	250.9
	1979	-44.4	1.1	45.5	52.9	57.9	5.0	-208.6	89.0	297.6	-200.1	148.0	348.1
	1980	-46.0	1.7	47.7	70.5	76.0	5.5	-239.2	111.3	350.5	-214.7	189.0	403.7
	1981	-37.2	1.4	38.6	66.9	74.2	7.3	-252.2	129.6	381.8	-222.5	205.2	427.7
	1982	-42.2	1.0	43.2	81.6	90.5	8.9	-257.3	109.1	366.4	-217.9	200.6	418.5
	1983	-37.9	1.1	39.0	59.1	65.9	6.8	-272.9	134.0	406.9	-251.7	201.0	452.7
	1984	-34.4	1.1	35.5	75.3	83.5	8.2	-263.2	99.9	363.1	-222.3	184.5	406.8
	1985	-37.3	1.0	38.3	60.6	69.3	8.7	-243.4	96.1	339.5	-220.1	166.4	386.5
	1986	-48.6	1.5	50.1	70.9	81.8	10.9	-280.8	156.0	436.8	-258.5	239.3	497.8
Gaza Area	1969	0.6	5.9	5.3	1.2	1.3	0.1	-18.8	2.7	21.5	-17.0	9.9	26.9
	1970	0.7	6.7	6.0	3.3	3.4	0.1	-23.9	4.6	28.5	-19.9	14.7	34.6
	1971	7.5	15.0	7.5	3.4	3.5	0.1	-32.0	9.5	41.5	-21.1	28.0	49.1
	1972	6.3	13.5	7.2	3.2	3.3	0.1	-41.9	15.2	57.1	-32.4	32.0	64.4
	1973	6.2	13.5	7.3	4.4	4.5	0.1	-51.0	25.1	76.1	-40.4	43.1	83.5
	1974	-2.3	12.2	14.5	9.3	9.4	0.1	-79.7	35.6	115.3	-72.7	57.2	129.9
	1975	4.1	13.5	9.4	16.8	17.0	0.2	-113.8	53.4	167.2	-92.9	83.9	176.8
	1976	-3.3	12.9	16.2	25.0	25.1	0.1	-103.7	66.1	169.8	-82.0	104.1	186.1
	1977	-4.8	12.0	16.8	44.4	44.4	0.0	-143.3	80.5	223.8	-103.7	136.9	240.6
	1978	-9.5	8.7	18.2	33.7	33.7	0.0	-106.8	79.9	186.7	-82.6	122.3	204.9
	1979	-15.1	9.3	24.4	34.2	34.2	0.0	-115.3	80.0	195.3	-96.2	123.5	219.7
	1980	-19.2	9.8	29.0	31.3	31.3	0.0	-118.8	113.1	231.9	-106.7	154.2	260.9
	1981	-19.4	7.5	26.9	31.2	31.2	0.0	-123.5	159.1	282.6	-111.7	197.8	309.5
	1982	-22.3	6.1	28.4	34.5	34.5	0.0	-132.6	149.4	282.0	-120.4	190.0	310.4
	1983	-19.4	7.0	26.4	22.5	22.5	0.0	-154.6	151.1	305.7	-151.5	180.6	332.1
	1984	-18.4	4.2	22.9	16.1	16.1	0.0	-161.0	95.8	256.8	-164.5	114.9	279.4
	1985	-18.2	4.7	22.9	16.1	16.1	0.0	-162.4	96.1	258.5	-164.5	116.9	281.4
	1986	-27.4	3.8	31.2	18.8	18.8	0.0	-210.4	133.1	343.5	-219.0	155.7	374.7

Source: Statistical Abstract of Israel, 1986. Judea, Samaria and Gaza Area Statistics, March, 1987

Employment

As stated earlier, the total employment of labor from the territories rose from 242,100 in 1985 to 261,200 in 1986, the largest increase (some 19,000) in many years (see Table 8). Much of this represented new entries into the labor force rather than a reduction in unemployment. This latter dropped from 3.6 percent to 3 percent (official figures)- a rate lower than Israel's rate. The increase in employment was 7.9 percent. Most of the increase (some 16,200 workers) were males.

The biggest increase occurred in employment in the West Bank which rose from 151,200 in 1985 to 167,000 in 1986 – an increase of some 15,800 or some 10.4 percent. Unemployment in the West Bank dropped from 5 percent to 3.8 percent. Participation in the labor force increased in 1986 from 34.8 percent (1985) to 36.1 percent (persons over the age of 14). Male participation in the labor force rose from 63.9 in 1985 to 66.7 percent in 1986.

In the Gaza Strip the increase was smaller – absolutely and proportionally – from 90,900 in 1985 to 94,200, an increase of some 3,300 workers. The entire increase was male workers (the number increased by 3,400). The official unemployment rate rose from 1.2 percent to 1.5 percent.

Of the 167,000 workers in the West Bank 115,700 or 69.3 percent were employed locally and another 51,300 or 30.7 percent were employed in Israel.

In the Gaza area of the 94,200 workers some 50,800 or 53.9 percent were employed locally and some 43,400 or 46.1 percent were employed in Israel.

The largest increase in labor employment in Israel occurred in the construction sector (3000 out of 5,500). The total percentage increase of West Bank/Gaza Strip employment in Israel was 6.2 percent. Of the 5,500 increase, 1,700 were from Gaza.

Table 9 shows the 1985 breakdown by sector and area of employment of labor from the territories. While 1986 data for Israeli employment (1,368,000) is available, the breakdown into Jews and Arabs has not been published yet so the 1985 data will be used to show the ethnic basis of employment in Israel. Labor from the territories accounted for 6.1 percent in 1985 and reached 6.5 percent in 1986. Taking population and labor growth rates into

TABLE 8

1985 WB/GS AND ISRAELI SECTORIAL AND ETHNIC EMPLOYMENT ANALYSIS[1]

	Agriculture		Industry[3]		Construction		Service[4]		Total	
	No. (000)	%	No. (000)	%	No. (000)	%	No. (000)	%	No. (000)	%
WB/GS										
1. WB/GS Residents Employed in WB/GS	37.2	24.4	24.6	16.1	16.9	11.1	74.0	48.4	152.7	100
2. WB/GS Residents Employed in Israel	13.9	15.6	15.9	17.8	42.4	47	17	19.1	89.2	100
3. Total WB/GS Employment	51.1	21.1	40.5	16.8	59.3	24.5	91	37.6	241	100
4. Percentage of WB/GS Labor Employed in Israel (2/3)	–	27.2	–	39.3	–	71.5	–	18.7	–	36.9
5. Percentage of Israel's Labor from WB/GS (2/10)	–	15.1	–	4.7	–	37	–	1.9	–	6.1
Israel										
6. Jewish Labor in Israel	62.5	5.1	293	24.2	43.2	3.6	814.9	67.1	1,213.6	100
7. Israeli Arab Labor in Israel	15.6	10.0	31.3	20.2	29.1	18.8	78.7	50.9	154.7	100
8. Total Israeli Labor in Israel(6/7)	78.1	5.7	324.3	23.7	72.3	5.3	893.6	65.3	1,368.3	100
9. Arab Labor in Israel	29.5	12.1	47.2	19.4	71.5	29.3	95.7	39.2	243.9	100
10. Total Employment in Israel (6/9)	92	6.3	340.2	23.3	114.7	7.9	910.6	62.5	1,457.5	100
11. Arab Labor in Israel as % of Labor in Israel (9/10)	–	29.5	–	13.9	–	62.3	–	10.5	–	16.7

1. Source: Central Bureau of Statistics, 1986, Jerusalem
2. Jewish Labor in WB/GS is only included in data on Israel
3. Industry includes manufacturing, handicrafts, electricity and mining
4. Services include all categories not covered elsewhere – both public and private

account, Arab labor (including Israeli Arabs) employed in Israel probably rose to 17.5 percent in 1986 (from 16.7 percent in 1985).

In 1985 Arab labor in construction reached 62.3 percent. By 1986 it was probably 65 percent of all construction labor. Of the manual labor in that sector it probably reached 80 percent.

Arab labor in Israeli agriculture represented 29.5 percent of employed in 1985, and probably exceeded 30 percent in 1986. Even in Israeli industry Arab employment approached 15 percent (1986).

Measured against the local consumer index, wages for West Bank residents increased by 12.7 percent in 1986 after a decline of 5.3 percent the previous year. For the Gaza workers wages increased even more – by some 20.6 percent in 1986 after a fall in 1985 of 12.7 percent. Nevertheless, the large differential with Israeli labor remains.

In 1986 61 percent of West Bank employed persons were employees, 36 percent self employed and a mere 3 percent employers. Twenty six percent of West Bank employed were illiterate, and 33 percent had 1-6 years of schooling (one third of total West Bankers employed in Israel). Forty three percent had 7-12 years of schooling, and 10 percent had 13+ years of schooling. Only 3 thousand West Bankers employed in Israel attended schools of higher education ("academics"). One third of West Bankers employed are unskilled laborers, 40 percent are semi-skilled and one quarter are white collar workers.

Agriculture

In the occupied territories 1985-1986 was a good agricultural year, mainly due to a record olive harvest. One hundred and fifty thousand tons of olives were harvested, compared to the previous record, attained in 1979-1980, of 120,000 tons. Even without the increase in olive output, the value of agricultural production rose by 13 percent compared to 1984-1985.

The territories' value of agricultural output reached US$600 million (US$500 million in the West Bank and 100 million in Gaza). It equalled 25 percent of Israel's value of agricultural products, compared to only 16 percent in 1984-1985. The Gaza Strip, however, suffered a decline of 2 percent. This was mainly

TABLE 9

WEST BANK-GAZA STRIP EMPLOYMENT ANALYSIS: 1986* (NO. IN THOUSANDS)

	West Bank		Gaza Strip		Total WB+GS	
	No.	%	No.	%	No.	%
Israel	51.3	30.7**	43.4	46.1**	94.7	36.3**
Agriculture	5.5	10.7	9.4	21.6	14.9	15.7
Industry	9.1	17.7	7.4	17.1	16.5	17.4
Construction	26	50.7	19.4	44.7	45.4	48
Services	10.7	20.9	7.7	16.6	17.9	18.9
West Bank/Gaza	115.7	69.3**	50.8	53.9**	166.5	63.7**
Agriculture	33	28.5	8.5	16.8	41.5	24.9
Industry	18.2	15.7	9	17.8	27.2	16.4
Construction	14.7	12.7	4.2	8.3	18.9	11.4
Services	49.8	43.1	29	57.1	78.8	47.3
Total	167	100	94.2	100	261.2	100
Agriculture	38.5	23.1	18	19.1	56.5	21.7
Industry	27.2	16.3	16.5	17.5	43.7	16.7
Construction	40.8	24.4	23.5	25	64.3	24.6
Services	60.5	36.2	36.2	38.4	96.7	37

* Source: Judea, Samaria and Gaza Area Statistics, March, 1987.

** These percentages refer to breakdown between Israel and the Territories. Rest of numbers in column refer to distribution by sectors and total 100%.

due to a 16 percent drop in citrus production, which is the mainstay of Gaza's agriculture.

These relatively favorable developments came after four years of decline in agricultural production, caused mainly by severe draughts. The effects of climatic conditions were manifested in a reduction of 20 percent in the area of rainfed arable land. This fell from 1,900,000 dunams in 1981 to 1,600,000 dunams in 1985. The total cultivated land fluctuated regularly according to climatic conditions, within the range of areas cultivated since 1968. The irrigated land, however, increased since 1980 by 13 percent, and reached 104,000 dunams, or over 6 percent of the total cultivated area. Almost all of the increase in irrigated land occurred in the Jordan Valley, and the main crop in the expanded irrigated areas was watermelon.

During the period under review, there has been a slight increase in the total value of purchased inputs, and especially in the purchase of agricultural machinery.

The balance of agricultural trade with Israel since 1982 remained, as noted, negative. This means, a surplus of imported produce from Israel, to the tune of US$16 million (6 percent of total import surplus). Agricultural exports, as a percentage of total exports, decreased from 49 percent in 1968 to 29 percent in 1985. The Gaza Strip, which in the past was a net exporter of agricultural produce has turned into a net importer.

Although the level of government subsidies and other institutional subsidies granted to Israeli farming has been markedly reduced in 1985-86, Palestinian farmers were still unable to compete with their Israeli counterparts. The level of direct subsidies for Israeli produce (milk, eggs and poultry) and the subsidy for water has decreased from US$1.5 billion in 1981 to 379 million US$ in 1987. Yet price stabilizing funds to marketing boards, government participation in an insurance fund for natural disasters, participation in export promotion funds, and market research remained in effect. Subsidy for water for irrigation remained 50 percent of the price. All of these incentives were not available to Palestinian farmers. Severe constraints exist on agricultural export to Jordan and to Europe. The bureaucratic and administrative inefficiencies in Jordan are severe, and the cost of transporting produce over the bridges is high. There is a limit on the volume of agricultural produce that can be exported to Jordan, and Jordanian officials visit the territories to set export quotas that cannot exceed 50 percent of the estimated produce. There are also Jordanian restrictions on the frequency of transport, which benefits East Bank farmers. Price is controlled by a Jordanian marketing company owned by the Jordanian government. Poor marketing, high costs of transportation and low prices cause Palestinian farmers to prefer the Israeli market and the European market, rather than the Jordanian.

Export of Palestinian agricultural produce to European markets is channelled through Israel's export marketing organization, Agrexco. Palestinians are opposed to the government decision which compels them to market exclusively through an organization owned by the Israeli farming establishment, and subsequently represents Israeli interests. They are adamant in their refusal to allow Israeli farmers to control their economic fate, and are politically opposed to the fact that their produce is exported under an Israeli brand name (Carmel). If they are compelled to market through Agrexco, they feel that they should also be provided with the same rights enjoyed by Israeli farmers. This would enable them to sell their produce in Israel without permits, just as Israeli farmers are able to sell in the territories. In addition, Palestinian farmers are also excluded from the extension assistance that helps Israeli farmers to introduce new export varieties and they are not integrated into the planning process which coordinates marketing and export.

EEC policy guidelines set at 1986, encourage marketing of Palestinian produce independent of Agrexco, and special quotas have been established, on concessional terms. The Israeli authorities have rejected that proposition, claiming that it will require duplication of marketing facilities, and unnecessary competition which will be harmful to both sectors. There have also been political objections, reflecting Israeli support of the Jordanian five year plan (see below) which is aimed at channelling all West European economic assistance through Jordan and preventing the development of an independent Palestinian economic sector. In May 1987 Palestinian farmers petitioned the Israeli High Court of Justice, and the case is still pending.

Industry

During the period under review, industrial production, revenues and sales to Israel and Jordan have increased, and contributed to the considerable growth in the West Bank/Gaza Strip GDP (see above). This improvement, which came after five years of stagnation, followed the up turn in the Israeli economy. This business cycle, which closely follows the fluctuations of the Israeli economy, points to the absolute dependence of West Bank industry upon Israel.

The improvement in industrial production has not cured the West Bank industry's basic malaise. The contribution of industry to West Bank GDP (value added), which was about 8 percent in 1986, was still lower than at the beginning of the occupation (9 percent). The total number employed in industry remained constant at 16,000-17,000 persons (excluding olive oil presses and stone quarries). The combined West Bank/Gaza Strip industrial production constituted a mere 1.4 percent of Israel's industry. A total value added of 2,500 enterprises was around US$ 80 million which is smaller than the output of some of Israel's larger industrial plants. West Bank industry is the least productive sector in the region's economy. Industrial value added per worker is 51 percent of average (West Bank) GDP per worker. Value added per worker in the West Bank is only 19 percent of Israel's productivity.

Food, beverages and tobacco contributed 46.6 percent to total industrial revenues.; rubber, plastic and chemical products – 15.9 percent; non-metallic materials – 8.0 percent; textiles and clothing 7.4 percent and metal products – 7.4 percent.

Almost one-third of the people employed in West Bank industry are self-employed in 1,200 establishments. Three hundred and fifty establishments employed 6,600 people. Annual average wages in Israel are four times as high as West Bank industrial wages. West Bank industry remains underdeveloped, small scale and traditional. With the exception of a few larger plants, there is no evidence of an emerging modern industrial sector. Bahiri (Bahiri S., Industrialization in the West Bank and Gaza Strip, WBDP and JP, 1987) explored the constraints on industrial development of the territories and recorded "economic, administrative, political and cultural" barriers which have resulted "in a continuation of the

TABLE 10

EXPORTS TO JORDAN, BY MAIN COMMODITY GROUPS, 1980-1986
(thousand U.S.$)

INDUSTRIAL PRODUCTS								AGRICULTURAL PRODUCE							
Other	Pickle Olives	Plastic Prod.	Stones	Marble	Soap	Olive Oil	Samna & Dairy Prod.	Total	Other	Vege-tables	Other Fruits	Citrus Fruit	Total	Grand Total	
2,772	2,620	324	3,482	1,369	4,432	28,548	15,239	58,786	86	3,231	7,569	37,627	48,513	107,299	1980
2,696	2,028	240	3,266	3,212	4,239	24,047	14,239	53,967	505	5,345	10,264	35,320	51,434	105,401	1981
2,242	2,300	291	1,859	6,425	4,288	20,311	19,016	56,732	387	9,276	14,214	44,336	68,267	124,999	1982
1,453	2,471	774	4,494	3,559	3,715	13,574	13,929	43,970	583	4,101	13,082	26,145	43,911	87,881	1983
1,391	1,492	439	5,662	4,967	3,552	26,949	17,670	62,122	600	5,244	12,584	17,849	36,276	98,398	1984
1,743	28	322	11,874	161	3,433	687	18,404	36,652	504	8,334	15,798	24,175	48,811	85,463	1985
1,531	2,387	519	11,669	149	3,651	22,306	15,802	58,014	1,124	4,905	13,476	23,089	42,594	100,608	1986

backward underdeveloped nature of industry – despite a relatively rapid rise in the consumption of industrial goods".

Some observers suggest that the constraints on industrial development are the result of a deliberate and consistent Israeli policy aimed at keeping the territories as a dumping ground for Israeli industrial produce and a pool of cheap labor. We have suggested elsewhere (The West Bank Handbook,WBDP and JP, 1986, p.67) that close scrutiny of the Israeli economic decision-making process shows that the "consistent" policy is merely a haphazard response to political pressure of concessions to Israeli economic pressure groups.

Economic and industrial stagnation has been determined by the political facts of occupation, the unequal relationship between the highly developed Israeli economy and the backward, traditional West Bank/Gaza Strip economy, and Israeli and Jordanian protectionist policies. A U.S. Aid study (Spector, B.I. *et.al.*, The Economic Implications of a Middle East Peace Settlement: An Economic Development Model for the West Bank and Gaza Strip, CACI US Aid, Washington DC, 1978) sums up the constraints on industrialization thus: "Political uncertainty; limited domestic markets for industrial products due to low purchasing power; lack of expertise, entrepreneurship and willingness to invest capital; out of date technology, low levels of education and vocational training; the absence of complementary services and developed infrastructure, including electricity; and the lack of adequate natural resources which results in an increase of the import of raw material".

Given the existing political impasse and the attempts at legitimizing the status-quo (see below), there is little chance that a more favorable climate for industrial development will be created.

The Jordanian Five Year Plan

In the summer of 1986, following the abrogation of the Hussein-Arafat agreement and the closure of PLO offices in Jordan, the Jordanian government has published a Five Year Program (1986-1990) for the Economic and Social Development of the Occupied Territories. The first draft put the total outlay of the plan at US$1.3 billion; in November 1986 the plan was scaled down to US$1.014

billion, and in May 1987 it was further reduced to just over US$900 million.

The stated objectives of the plan and the criteria determining priorities have also changed since it was first published. The first draft defined the primary objective as: "Limiting the emigration of the (occupied territories) population, especially permanent emigration, while also minimizing the temporary emigration motivated by work or study needs". The criteria for priorities stated economic actions that will have "effects on the Arab village and rural life and their attraction as places of work and raising families in competition with urban life and opportunities". Following criticism that the plan's main objectives are, therefore, to protect the East Bank from an influx of Palestinians, and to gain influence among rural and traditional Palestinians against PLO, radical centers in towns, the Jordanians were prompted to alter the prime objectives to "enhance the ability of both citizens and institutions, to resist and withstand the occupiers' persistent efforts, to destroy their national identity and uproot them from their land".

The detailed blueprint, which specifies the various projects in the West Bank and Gaza is very sketchy. Of the total projects listed for the West Bank, only 26 percent (US$116.5 m.) out of almost $450 million) are allocated to identifiable projects. Almost all projects in the Gaza Strip are classified by sectors, but are unspecified geographically. Some projects (especially cooperative housing) are very detailed, but others are general and merit two lines of description. The distribution of the specified projects by regions (in the West Bank) is illuminating. Almost half of these projections are located in the Hebron area, 10.0 percent in Nablus, 15.5 percent in Bethlehem, 7.4 percent in Jerusalem and 12.5 percent in the Ramallah – al Bira area.

The plan allocates one third of the total to individual salaries, mortgages and grants, 31.5 percent to social services, 13.7 percent to production (agriculture, industry); 11.8 percent to physical infrastructure; and 7.8 percent to financing. Planned capital investment by sectors is: housing 55 percent; physical infrastructure 16.2 percent; industry and agriculture 18 percent. In agriculture the emphasis is on livestock and land reclamation. Industrial development is aimed at developing traditional labor-intensive enterprises: two thirds to food industries, 14 percent to souvenirs and only 10 percent to pharmaceutics. There is no attempt to develop high-tech industries or any other capital-intensive enterprises. Electricity gets 3.0 percent of the budget and water 5.4 percent.

The economic development guidelines are, in effect, the continuation of the pre-1967 Jordanian economic strategy for the West Bank. This puts an emphasis on agricultural development and tourism (and related industries) but no serious development of advanced industries or related infrastructure (electrification). There is a strong emphasis on rural development and a bias against urban needs.

The "educational doctrine" defined in the plan is to prepare "manpower to function independently from support by the public sector or private institutions virtually in a free enterprise highly competitive situation". This is a remarkable statement considering the existing unfair competition experienced by Palestinian farmers and other entrepreneurs in their dealings with Israelis and Jordanians. It serves, however, the purpose of allocating the lion's share of the assistance to the private and commercial sector, and relatively small amounts to the public Palestinian sector (controlled by the PLO). Vast amounts are allocated to salaries, individual grants and mortgages, as well as the channelling of the funds through pro-Jordanian personalities and Jordanian controlled institutions (cooperatives, banks). This indicates that the Jordanians are determined to maintain the system of patronage, thus combatting PLO influence.

The Jordanian Five Year Plan pursue policies similar to the Israeli economic-political strategy in the occupied territories i.e.- development of the rural sector and curbing the influence of the PLO. Therefore, the Israelis have responded favorably to the plan, and Israeli officials solicited contributions to it in Western countries. Table 11 compares Israeli capital investment in the occupied territories based on 4 years (1984-1987) and Jordanian capital investment plan (1986-1990).

The mechanism through which the Jordanians sought to implement the Five Year Plan is the Cairo-Amman Bank, the second largest bank in Jordan. It is the only bank partially owned by the government. The plan makes ample references to the need

TABLE 11
ISRAELI AND JORDANIAN CAPITAL INVESTMENT JORDAN (PLAN 1986-90), ISRAEL (DEVELOPMENT BUDGETS 1984-87) US$ (000,000)

Sector	Jordan	%	Israel	%
Financial inst.	77.3	15.2	–	–
Agriculture	75.6	14.8	1.2	1.0
Industry	68.7	13.5	–	–
Electricity	15.7	3.0	5.2	4.3
Roads	18.6	3.6	11.5	9.4
Water	27.0	5.4	9.0	7.3
Sewerage (Gaza)	25.5	5.0	–	–
Unspecified Infrastructure	37.5	7.4	36.0	29.5
School Const.	60.7	11.9	12.3	10.1
Welfare	25.2	4.9	0.8	0.6
Health	78.2	15.3	23.3	19.1
Post,Phones	–	–	12.3	10.1
Offices	–	–	1.0	0.9
Tourism	–	–	0.9	0.7
Transport (buses)	–	–	0.6	0.5
Misc.	–	–	7.9	6.5
Total	510.0	100.0	122.0	100.0

to establish, or re-open specialized financial institutions, which will be "totally Jordanian and subject to Jordan's competence ... the majority of the equity of such institutions must belong to the Jordanian government and public sector corporation".

Israeli and Jordanian representatives, working in full cooperation with US officials, signed an agreement which stipulates a system of shared control over the Bank by the Israeli Central Bank and the Jordanian Royal Bank. The first branch of the Cairo-Amman Bank was opened in Nablus in the fall of 1986, and by mid- 1987 more than 1,000 accounts have been opened. The Bank, however, has difficulty providing credit facilities, due to the lack of sufficient funds and collaterals.

Lack of funds characterizes the initial phase of implementation of the Five Year Plan. Out of US$200 million planned, only less than US$60 million has been available. Jordan allocated US$30 million. The US government, Great Britain and France provided approximately US$25 million. Saudi Arabia paid the last installment on money pledged to the joint PLO-Jordanian committee, on the condition that it will be distributed jointly by the PLO and Jordan. An additional US$11.5 million has been allocated to private voluntary agencies operating in the area.

UNRWA spends some US$75 million annually in the refugee camps. A reasonable estimate of total public expenditure and investment in the occupied territories during 1987-1988 is as follows:

Israeli Civilian Administration	US$260 million
Jordanian Government and foreign countries	US$75 million
UNRWA	US$75 million

Out of the total US$410 million, one quarter is for capital investment. It should be pointed out in this context that the annual capital investment in the Israeli sector (settlements) had been, since 1984, more than US$150 million (see Table 18).

The significance of the Jordanian Five Year Plan lies in the realm of politics rather than in economics. That aspect will be discussed below (Section Four).

Public Expenditure and Investment

Public expenditure expresses in monetary terms the level of services provided to the inhabitants. Public investment (capital formation) is the development expenditure on creating physical infrastructure and other fixed assets. Both items are represented in the regular and development budgets of the Military Government (Civilian Administration) and of the local (Palestinian) authorities. They do not include expenditure for maintenance and capital investment in the Jewish sector (settlements), described below. The share of public expenditure (consumption) in the uses of the local Palestinian population is described above (Table 6). During the period under review it remained below 7 percent of West Bank resources and 6 percent of Gaza Strip resources. This low rate does not meet the growth demands of the economy and indicates a very low level of services.

There has been a 13.5 percent increase in the regular budget of the civilian administration in the West Bank, from US$126.7 million in 1986 to US$143.4 million in 1987, and an increase of 26 percent in the regular budget of the Gaza Strip, from US$52.4

million in 1986 to US$66.0 million in 1987. The authorities point out that actual expenditure is usually higher than budgets. They expect that in 1987, actual expenditure will be US$40 million higher than the sums allocated in the budget. There has been no substantial change in the composition of the regular budget (salaries, activities, etc.) and the relative allocations to different departments (education, health, public works, etc., see 1986 Report p.15). The ratio of maintenance (regular) versus investment (development) outlay remained unaltered, roughly 80 percent maintenance and 20 percent development (approved budgets).

An analysis of Civilian Government actual development spending (as opposed to budgetary allocations) is presented in table 12.

TABLE 12
CIVILIAN ADMINISTRATION CAPITAL INVESTMENT 1983-1987
(fiscal years)
(in mill. US$)

Year	West Bank	Gaza	Total	Annual increase %
1983	24.0	11.0	35.0	-
1984	21.0	7.0	28.0	(-)20.0
1985	38.0	11.0	49.0	(+)75.0
1986	56.0	26.0	82.0	87.8
1987(budget)	31.2	13.7	44.9	-
Total	170.2	68.7	238.9	

Between 1985 and 1987 larger sums were allocated to water works, school construction (almost doubled in 1987), telephones and health (almost quadrupled). Loans and grants to Palestinian local authorities almost doubled.

In Gaza, loans and grants to Palestinian local authorities tripled, and health development doubled.

Total development budgets (1984-1987) in the West Bank were distributed as follows: 21.0 percent local authorities; 21.0 percent health; 12.7 percent road construction; 12.2 percent telephone grids; 10.7 percent water works; 7.0 percent school construction; 6.2 percent electricity. In Gaza, 47.2 percent was allocated to Palestinian local authorities; 16.8 percent to school construction; 14.7 percent to health; 4.8 percent to telephone grids.

The overall level of the Civilian Government annual spending in the occupied territories remained constant since 1984, around US$250-280 million. The share of "local revenues" rose from 58 percent in 1983 to 82 percent in 1987 (as estimated in the budget books). In mid-May 1987, Israeli officials stated that in the fiscal year 1987-88 local revenues will cover the entire outlay and there will be no further need to cover deficits of the "closed budgetary system" of the occupied territories by transferring Israeli budgetary allocations.

The Civilian Administration stated officially that they "do not demand any Israeli government contributions to their budget", and that the present level of public expenditure and investment is the maximum they can use. These statements indicate that the level of services, and development projects that have been attained in 1985-1987 seem to the Israeli authorities satisfactory and meet the needs of the Palestinian population. It should be pointed out in that context, that per capita public consumption (civilian only) in Israel was US$1,350 in 1985, and per capita public consumption in the territories, only US$185 per capita, or 13.7 percent of the Israeli level.

Fiscal Burden

The attitude of avoiding any undue fiscal burden on the Israeli taxpayer, emanating from the Civilian Administration activities, seems reasonable had it not been based on misleading facts.

The occupied territories never constituted a fiscal burden on the Israeli treasury. On the contrary, the Palestinian population contributed large sums to the Israeli public consumption. In the past, part of those contributions (described below) were returned to the territories to cover the Civilian Government's deficit. In 1986 total Palestinian contributions have been retained by the Israeli treasury.

Palestinian contributions are composed of taxes and other deductions imposed upon Palestinians employed officially in Israel. They are also composed of indirect taxes, such as duties on Palestinian goods imported through Israeli ports and value added tax on commodities and services purchased in Israel by Palestinian inhabitants residing in the territories. To arrive at the net fiscal contribution of Palestinians under occupation to the Israeli treasury (excluding local taxation), however, one should deduct subsidies on Israeli subsidized products consumed in the territories.

The main source of direct fiscal income to the Israeli treasury is the "deduction fund" created by an Israeli cabinet decision on October 8, 1970. Its aim had been to "ensure conditions of fair competition" between Palestinian and Israeli workers. The decision stipulated that "taxes, deductions and social benefits that Israeli workers were enjoying will be handled in the same fashion as in Israel. The balance of funds and social benefits will be transferred to a Deduction Fund. The fund will assist in developing social services in the territories".

Since 1970, large sums composed of 20 percent of the workers' pay, and employers contribution to social benefits, are collected by the Government Employment Service from all Palestinians working officially in Israel. However, whereas for the Israeli worker, payments are transferred to the National Insurance Institute and accrued on his behalf; those made in the name of the Palestinian worker are transferred directly to the treasury. As National Insurance applies only to Israeli territory (and Israeli settlers) the Palestinian worker is not entitled to insurance, except when staying in Israel proper. For example, childbirth benefits and 12 weeks paid maternity leave apply only if Palestinian women give birth in an Israeli hospital, which seldom occurs. A Palestinian worker is not entitled to payments for old age, widowhood, dependent children, survivors, general disability, unemployment (all covered by National Insurance) despite the fact that sums were deducted from his salary.

The size of the Deduction Fund has not been revealed, despite repeated requests by Israeli and international bodies. According to our own estimates, the sums accrued in the Fund since 1970 exceed US$800 million, and with a modest (compounded) interest, exceed US$1 billion. Three quarters of this sum were returned to the territories as contributions to the deficit of the Military Government, but at least US$250 million were retained by the treasury and used for Israeli public consumption. It should be noted in this context, that the entire Military Government (Civilian Administration) capital investment in the West Bank during twenty years of occupation came to US$400 million or 20 million average annual at current prices (data culled from annual budgets of the Military Government 1967-1987).

In an earlier publication we estimated the indirect taxes paid to Israel "proper" (VAT, fuel excise and import duties) in 1985 at $80 million, (VAT – $60 million, fuel excise – $16 million and import duties $5 million). If subsidies on Israeli food stuff is deducted the net indirect fiscal contribution is about US$50 million a year. The "occupation tax" that West Bankers and Gazans paid to the occupation authorities (excluding local taxes) during 20 years can be, therefore, estimated at a conservative figure of US$800 million. In 1987 alone, when the Civilian Government budget became "balanced", at least US$80 million of Palestinian contributions were directed to Israeli public expenditure. Israeli officials assert that the "the government is interested in contributing more to develop the quality of life in the territories, however, budgetary constraints in Israel are known to all", and therefore "foreign countries and international organization are encouraged to invest in assisting the territories". The 1986-87 "occupation tax" could have doubled the territories' development budget of that year.

THREE: LEGAL AND ADMINISTRATIVE DEVELOPMENTS

Palestinian Sector

Legislative activity of the Military Government was relatively limited during 1986-1987. Primary legislation (military orders) enacted during the period added 40 new orders (the latest, Order 1194, May 1987), as well as numerous appointments, mainly concerned with re-appointing Palestinian municipal committees (see below).

Two lists of censored publications (amendments No.76-77) added 74 books to the existing list of over 600 items. Amongst the publications banned are Islamic fundamentalist items, antisemitic works and nationalist-Palestinian fiction and poetry.

The bulk of the military orders deal with fiscal and economic matters. The most important amongst them is Order 1180, published in connection with the re-opening of the Cairo-Amman Bank in Nablus (see above), and instructions concerning banking (liquid assets) No. 5/86.

Order 1180 grants the Israeli comptroller of Banks (of the Bank of Israel) the right to issue directives concerning membership of the bank's executive body, its size (not exceeding 15) and the agenda considered by it. The comptroller is empowered to halt, in case of emergency, the operations of the bank for specific periods. Article 34 (amendment to the original Jordanian law 94/1966) states that the comptroller may exempt from the provisions of this law, or any part thereof, any licensed bank, which is a branch of a bank registered in Israel, and which operates in accordance with Israeli laws. Based on that article, the comptroller, indeed, issued "liquidity instructions" which exempt Israeli banks operating in the territories (article 16) from these instructions. The local bank must keep the liquid assets in the Bank of Israel. Deposits in Jordanian dinars must not exceed a ceiling determined by the comptroller, and if it does, the bank must keep against dinar deposits dinar banknotes to the full amount of the deposits.

There has been no substantial change in actual administrative arrangements, with the exception of the return of Palestinian mayors to all West Bank municipalities, following an agreement reached between Israel and Jordan (see Section Four). The separation of Israeli and Palestinian administrative systems has been further enhanced by the establishment of a Motor Vehicle Registration office in Ariel for the exclusive use of Israeli settlers, and a branch of the National Insurance Institute in which West Bank Palestinians are not eligible to enroll. The Civilian Government divided the function of staff officer for the interior (responsible for local authorities and planning) and appointed one officer for the Jewish local authorities and another for Arab local authorities (and planning).

Data Bank

The most significant change in the authorities' mode of operation is of seemingly technical nature. The Ministry of Defense has created, with an investment of US$8.5 million, a computerized Data Bank of the territories. The stated objective is to computerize all Civilian Administration functions and all information pertaining to the population: property, real estate, family ties, political attitudes, involvement in illegal activities, licensing, occupations, consumption patterns, etc. The authorities will gain "complete control in real-time of all information on the territories, which will ensure strategic control and improvement of services".

Due to the "sensitive nature" of the project, only Israeli computer firms were allowed to participate in the bid. A local firm, TIM, representing Data General (a U.S. computer company), won the bid, for which huge U.S. firms, such as IBM and Digital, also competed through local representatives. To ensure secrecy, the programing is done by Ministry of Defense programmers. The project became operational in August 1987. It is connected to the Gaza Strip project, computerizing 16 Arab local councils and Civilian Administration functions, and the computerization of 25 West Bank municipalities.

Civilian Administration officials describe the project as "vital, to provide services to the population", but do not hide the "population control" aspect. It is indeed, the ultimate instrument of population control, a computerized carrot-and-stick operation. By pressing a key on a computer terminal, any Civilian Administration official will gain access to name-lists of "positives" and "hostiles", and decide on the fate of their applications, from car licensing to water quotas, import permits and travel documents. "Black Lists" have been for a long time an important element of the "reward and punishment" system. The Data Bank might, however, develop into a sinister "big brother" control apparatus in the hands of an administration that already possesses absolute power and is free of any checks and balances. The potential peril to basic human rights, protection of privacy, and norms of natural justice should not be underestimated. The computerization project, if allowed to attain its stated goals, may prove to be a mile-stone in the institutionalization of the ultimate police-state in the territories.

Physical Planning and Land Ownership

The separate planning process, one for the Israeli settlements and the other for Palestinians, initiated in the late seventies continued under separate administrations, different standards, and with clear efforts to use physical planning as a tool in the scramble for control over space.

The planning process in the Israeli settlements was devolved, with the participation of all Israeli national planning and building authorities, and local and regional settlers' councils. By mid-1987 274 statutory plans for Jewish built-up areas had been processed. Eighty six plans were approved, 110 have been "deposited" and 78 are pending approval (some awaiting legal opinion on land ownership). The Israeli State Comptroller, who in 1984 criticized the settlements' planning process, reiterated his remarks in 1986. The physical plans for settlements encompassed tens of thousands of dunams. All planning criteria and standards (densities, infrastructure, public institutions) complied with Israeli standards. The legal process remained, however, Jordanian (town and village planning law, 1966, as amended by military orders).

In the Palestinian sector the planning process remained haphazard, irregular and disorderly. In 1979, a private Israeli planner was commissioned to prepare physical plans for 180 villages, and in 1984, 103 villages were added. The village schemes were based on faulty and inaccurate surveys (demographic and physical) and were therefore shelved. In 1986 the Civilian Administration commissioned Israeli and Palestinian planners to prepare schemes for 55 villages. Master plans for 20 towns were also commissioned. Palestinian planners, who previously refused to participate in the planning process have increasingly accepted planning assignments for Palestinian localities. This change has occurred as a result of Jordanian efforts to engage in physical planning in the occupied territories.

The Five Year Development Plan (see above) has allocated US$3 million for regional and development plans and an additional US$10 million for master planning and detailed planning of towns and villages. Local planning offices have already received large sums from Jordan which are matched by Civilian Administration contributions. All planning assignments must be approved by both governments.

By 1987 not a single scheme had passed the initial phase of approval ("deposition for objections") except the Beit Jallah master plan. The State Comptroller observed, in his 1986 report, that it seems the planning authorities prefer to retain a free hand in granting building licenses. Approval of binding planning documents would secure building rights of Palestinian residents and make them less dependent on the Israeli authorities. The authorities, however, are determined to use planning as an instrument of punishment and reward for political and security purposes.

It should be recalled that Military Order 418 (March 1971) transferred all planning powers to the High Planning Committee made up entirely by Israeli officials and except within municipal boundaries (see below) all building licenses (in more than 400 villages) have been granted exclusively by the "High Committee".

In July 1986 a major scandal, involving bribery and other irregularities was revealed. It involved Israeli officials responsible for planning and licensing in the Arab sector, as well as Palestinian officials and building inspectors. The officials were indicted and removed from their jobs, but were not replaced. Since January (1987) therefore, no building license has been granted to Palestinian residents in the West Bank.

The Civilian Administration expanded the municipal boundaries of Palestinian towns including Nablus (from 18,000 to 25,000 dunams) and Jenin (to 5,500 dunams), following the expansion of Hebron (in 1984) and other smaller towns. The expanded boundaries affected only privately owned Arab lands and especially excluded "state lands", as those are considered reserved for exclusive Jewish usage.

The legal process of "declaration of state lands" (1986 report p.27) has slowed down considerably. A survey of the Civilian Administration showed that 300,000 dunams (out of a total 2.15 million dunams) located and mapped as potential "state land" (i.e. not registered and uncultivated) cannot be "declared" due to "illegal Arab cultivation" or other reasons. Therefore, the maximum size of "declared" state land *should be reduced to 1.85 mllion, from 39 percent of the West Bank area to 34 percent, and the total area under exclusive Israeli control – from 41 percent to 36 percent (including land acquisitions and "military requisitions").*

Following the 1985 land scam (1986 Report p.35), there have been only a few land transactions, and the official (Government-Jewish National Fund) Acquisition Committee has been inactive.

Israeli Sector

During the period under review 4 additional Jewish local councils had been incorporated (Givat Ze'ev, Emmanuel, Alfei Menashe, Kokhav Yair), bringing the number to 10. The separate legislation for Jewish areas and residents had been expanded, and a new codex, holding 332 pages of orders, regulations and announcements had been published by the Legal Adviser for Judea and Samaria.

Israeli primary legislation concerning Jewish enclaves and personal status of settlers is based on laws enacted in the Knesset, and on military orders enacted by the Military Commander which copy verbatim Israeli legislation. A tangled system of secondary legislation, regulations, "announcements" and extra-legal arrangements have ensured that Israeli settlers moving to the occupied territories carry with them their personal and communal status. Although they have, in a legal sense, settled outside the borders of Israel and are subject to West Bank law (Jordanian law and security enactments).

Thus, in a series of laws and emergency regulations, the Knesset has established that for the purpose of certain basic laws Israelis or those entitled to Israeli citizenship through the Law of Return (i.e. Jews), would be viewed as residents of Israel.

However, the full scale of judicial ingenuity, in applying Israeli laws and norms to Jewish enclaves, is manifested by following the maze of military enactments on all levels, primary, secondary and tertiary.

Orders 783 (March 1979) and 892 (March 1981) stipulate that the IDF commander in the area is empowered to determine by regulations, guidelines for managing regional councils, and to establish directives concerning powers and administrative arrangements concerning the management of the affairs of "residents of the councils". For that purpose, the commander is empowered to establish a court for local affairs whose jurisdiction, and the laws by which it adjudicates will be determined in regulations (Articles 2,A,B).

Based on that "primary" legislation, detailed "regulations", copying almost verbatim Israeli local authorities ordinances have been issued. Thus, Israeli municipal laws have been introduced to the West Bank and apply only to Jewish enclaves, disguised as routine Military Government secondary legislation and signed by a low level "official responsible".

Chapter 16 of the "Regulations" deals with a Court of Law for Local Affairs. Article 140A in that chapter stipulates that the IDF Commander in the area is authorized to delegate powers and to appoint persons to act on his behalf (in the settlements), provided that the authorization and the enactments on which it is based are published in Annexes to the Regulations.

Based on Article 140A, a number of "annexes" have been issued. In Annex 1, "welfare enactments", two Israeli laws are specified and authorization is granted to "whoever is authorized in Israel". In Annex 2, one Israeli enactment concerning statistics is mentioned. Annex 3, "Personal Status" enactment, lists seven Israeli laws, and a number of Israeli officials are authorized to act according to Israeli laws. Annex 4, "Education Enactments" mentions four Israeli laws and authorizes to act those authorized to act in Israel. Annex 5, "Health Enactments" specifies ten Israeli laws and empowers all those empowered in Israel to act in the enclaves. Annex 6, "Labor Enactments", specifies four Israeli laws and authorizes Israeli officials to act accordingly. Thus, as "annexes" to "regulations" issued by virtue of "military orders", twenty eight Israeli laws and the entire administrative system based on them had been applied to the Jewish enclaves in the territories. A "decision", issued by the Director General of the Ministry of Education, "attached to annex 4", incorporates West Bank Jewish settlements into the administrative (Israeli) districts of the Ministry, and thus closes the circle.

FOUR: CONFRONTATIONS AND ATTITUDES

Violence

The quantifiable facts present an accurate picture of the intensity of the inter-communal strife in the occupied territories. Between April 1986 and May 1987, 3,150 incidents of violent demonstrations occurred, of which 1,870 incidents were of rockthrowing, 600 of stone roadblocks and burning tyres, and 665 incidents of Palestinian flag hoisting, leaflet distribution and slogan painting. During the same period, 65 incidents occurred, involving firearms, explosives, stabbings and 150 involving petrol bombs. Twenty two Palestinians were killed and 67 injured in violent incidents (seven killed by the army during demonstrations). Two Israelis were killed and 62 injured. Almost three thousand Palestinian demonstrators and 1,550 accused of terrorism were detained (April 1986-May 1987). In April 1987 alone, 109 Palestinians were detained without trial. Al-Haq, a Palestinian legal research institute in Ramallah supplied the following figures for Administrative orders during 1984-87:

	1984	1985	1986	1987(May)
Deportation orders (incl. Gaza)	1	31	5	4
Administrative Detention orders	0	131	37	62
Town Arrest orders	46	31	62	40
Houses demolished or sealed	4?	55	48	22

The intensity of violence in 1986-87 was less severe than in 1985-86 (4,000 disturbances, 139 terrorist attacks) but, the cycle which started in 1981-82 (4,400 incidents) remained for five consecutive years (1982-87) above the 3,000 mark. By comparison, the average annual occurrence of "disturbances" between 1977-82, was only 500.

The relationship between planned violent acts involving firearms, perpetrated by organized terrorist cells, and disturbances involving spontaneous rockthrowing and violent demonstrations indicate a new trend in Palestinian resistance. The ratio of terrorist/ spontaneous acts was 1:11 between 1977-84, 1:16 in 1985, 1:18 in 1986. This ratio indicates a new phase in Palestinian resistance and the inter-communal strife. Violence is largely carried out in broad daylight by individuals and groups who spontaneously express their feelings, undeterred by the consequence of their actions. Local initiative, rather than externally controlled violence, as an expression of resistance, is evident also from the type of weapons used. In 1985, there were 34 incidents of shooting by Palestinians and 12 hand-grenade attacks. In 1986 there were 18 shootings and 7 grenades, and in 1987 there were 12 and 6 respectively. By contrast, there were no cases of stabbing (which does not require smuggling of arms) in 1985, but 14 cases in 1986 and 13 in 1987. Security sources attribute the shift in type of violence to external reasons, notably the closure of PLO offices in Amman (1986), and the tightening of security measures on the borders (Lebanon, Jordan). However, there is no doubt about the grass-root origin of most violent actions.

The number and severity of retaliatory attacks by Jewish vigilantes has also risen. These involve gunfire, smashing windshields of parked Arab vehicles, burning houses and beating up passers-by. The most severe incidents occurred in the spring of 1987, in Kalkilya (following the death of a woman caused by a petrol bomb) and in the Deheishe refugee camp.

Settler vigilantes activity became more audacious due to the fact that perpetrators had not been punished. In many cases, settlers refused to obey orders of Israeli officers to refrain from passing roadblocks or to desist from committing hooliganism. Soldiers and officers were bodily harmed.

Ironically, all settlers belong to the security forces, being an integral part of the Israeli army (Territorial Defense Units). It is estimated that the settler population possesses no less than 10,000 firearms of all types, as well as other military equipment such as wireless sets and vehicles. The extreme ideological outlook shared by the settlers and their relative independence in defining their military role must lead to excesses. Moreover, military and police authorities are reluctant to prosecute vigilantes even when illegal operations, aimed against official government decisions, are perpetrated.

The political clout of the settlers, and the authorities' willingness to appease them was manifested in May 1987. Following a murderous attack on an Israeli civilian car, in which a woman and a child were burned to death, the settlers demanded from the government an "appropriate reprisal". They handed over a list of measures, which included mass arrest of prominent Palestinian leaders, closure of universities and curfews. That list was published in January 1987 by a body calling itself "Citizens for Yesha (Judea, Samaria and Gaza)", and rejected by the security authorities. In May, however, the Defense Ministry submitted to the pressure and carried out the entire settlers' list, including the arrest of 109 Palestinians. Military sources admitted later, that those harsh measures were uncalled for, because the incident was perpetrated by local groups with no contact with central PLO activists.

Another very important indicator for measuring the level of confrontation is the record number of Palestinian demonstrators killed by the security forces. Official figures put the number of Palestinians killed during 1987 at 22, compared with 8 in 1986. The authorities admit only 7 killings from army shooting, but fail to count at least 7 additional Palestinians shot dead "in uncertain circumstances". These presumably involve illegal shooting by settlers or stray bullets shot during disturbances. The tragic increase in the number of Palestinian casualties can be explained by the violent nature of the demonstrations, especially on university campuses where students were ready to risk their lives in confrontations with the soldiers, but also by the notorious "procedure of detention of suspects". This procedure, altered the earlier "orders regarding opening fire", which specified that "it is forbidden (to open fire) for the purpose of imposing public order or quelling riots". The new order permits opening fire "as part of procedure of detention of suspects during a disturbance". "Disturbance" is defined as – riots, demonstrations, gatherings, roadblocks. Opening fire is then permitted if "disturbance is followed by physical attack or rockthrowing or other 'cold' objects (i.e. iron-bars)". In such cases the soldier should "warn the suspect in a loud voice of his intention to open fire (in Arabic)". If the suspect was not apprehended, or tried to escape, it is permitted to open fire, first in "the air at an 80-degree angle upwards, then, with intent to injure, but only at the legs".

The definition of "demonstration" as a crime that permits soldiers to detain suspects; the permission to open fire against rockthrowers; the unclear definition of "warning in a loud voice", especially during a noisy encounter of hundreds of soldiers and demonstrators; the permission to use live ammunition by inexperienced conscripts; the fact that Palestinian youth have increasingly chosen to defy the soldiers – were all factors that brought about the dramatic increase in casualty figures. Along with it, they brought about the heightening of animosity and calls for revenge.

The violence of the 1986-87 period occurred in three major waves. The first, in December 1986, came after a period of relative calm. It began with a confrontation between soldiers and students at Bir-Zeit University that resulted in the death of two students. Demonstrations, stone throwing, and petrol bombs followed for the next week, spilling over to Gaza as well. When the violence finally ceased, two other Palestinian boys were dead, one possibly killed by the bullet of a settler. Scores were injured, including a sixty-one year old Israeli man stabbed in the Old City, and over a hundred Palestinians were arrested. Official government claims suggested the demonstrations were organized by the PLO rather than being a spontaneous response to the deaths at Bir Zeit. The Prime Minister at that time, Shimon Peres, maintained, however, that despite the disturbances, West Bank residents had experienced a major shift in loyalties, turning from PLO support to a pro-Jordanian position (see below).

In February 1987, the second period of unrest erupted (primarily in Gaza), in response to the deportation of a Khan Yunis student accused of leading the Fatah Youth Movement (Shabiba) in the area. It was fueled by the death of a Gazan teenager shot by the border police after resisting arrest for a stone throwing incident. It later spread to the Balata refugee camp near Nablus where residents held a general strike to protest a recent security crackdown. Four people were injured in a clash with soldiers, and when the news spread to the nearby A-Najah university, an impromptu demonstration was staged. Further demonstrations broke out throughout the territories which were seen by senior IDF officers as a deliberately organized response to the plight of besieged Palestinian refugee camps in Lebanon. Calm was restored only after all five West Bank universities were closed.

Begun as a show of support for a hunger strike waged by Palestinian security prisoners, the third outbreak of violence followed closely on the heels of the previous one. Sit-ins staged at Red Cross offices in major West Bank towns, occasionally turned into demonstrations which prompted border police and IDF involvement. After almost a week of such uprisings, an Israeli woman and child were burned to death by a petrol bomb. Settler riots in the town of Kalkilya followed, with cars and fields burned and windows smashed, including those of the mayor's home. Increased military presence, administrative detentions, curfews, roadblock, and deportations restored, for the time being, a semblance of order.

The increased number of spontaneous, individual acts by both settlers and Palestinians, indicated higher frustration levels of the civilian populations. Therefore,the task of the defense forces to keep order became more difficult. This form of violence and the accompanying military actions revealed contradictions in statements of Israeli politicians. On the one hand, Shimon Peres claimed that the local population has shifted its loyalties from the PLO to Jordan, thus increasing support for the policy of power sharing with Jordan (see below). On the other hand, outbreaks of violence were credited by the Ministry of Defense to PLO directives. The Israeli authorities might be better served by accepting the violence as individual and spontaneous acts emanating from a growing sense of despair and frustration. This requires the recognition that the problem is no longer limited to breaking up organized terrorist cells, but has evolved into population control. In other words, the conflict can no longer be maintained militarily as its political implications demand increased attention. Though the overwhelming majority support the nationalist stances of the PLO, the Palestinian population is now acting of its own accord.

Public Opinion Poll

Further evidence of an inherent, internally generated struggle emerged from a survey of political attitudes of Palestinians in the territories. This was conducted by a research team from a-Najah University in Nablus and sponsored by al-Fajr, an East Jerusalem paper, Newsday (Long Island, USA), and the Australian Broadcasting Company.

Among the most surprising results were that 93.5 percent of the respondents believe the PLO is the sole and legitimate representative of the Palestinian people, and the preferred leader is Yassir Arafat (71.1 percent), as opposed to 3.4 percent favoring King Hussein. Some 78.4 percent believe that acts of violence are justified in the pursuit of the Palestinian cause. Justification was given to the 1978 hijacking of an Israeli bus on the Tel-Aviv – Haifa highway by 87.6 percent of the respondents, placing a bomb on an Israeli El-Al plane by 60.5 percent, and the December 1985 attack against passengers in Vienna and Rome airports by 36.9 percent. The operative term in this question was "justified" and therefore, does not imply an overall terrorist population or mentality, but rather an environment within which terrorism can flourish.

Among those Israelis wishing to believe in reduced support for the PLO and a turn toward the favour of Israeli-Jordanian cooperation, the poll was dismissed as biased on the grounds that respondents were influenced by the interviewers, whom they described as Fatah activists. Indeed, one can argue that there were some biases in the survey. For example, 13 percent of those polled were in the professional/white collar category whereas in the CBS Statistics of Employed Persons, this group constitutes only 3-5 percent of the population. Some 13.9 percent of the sample were illiterate as opposed to 25 percent of the population; only 5 percent listed their place of work as Israel though in actuality, the number is about 37 percent. Therefore, the poll is a representation of the more politically active, professional segment of the society. Still, if one assumes the poll represents the opinions of the political elite, the results are quite significant.

In response to charges that interviewers intimidated the respondents, one would have to say that if the masses are so frightened as to be forced into these responses, this in itself would be an example of the strength of the PLO in the territories. Secondly, at each home people were asked if they wanted to participate in the survey. If they refused, the interviewer went to another home.

One must consider that the survey was done after twenty years of life under occupation and at a time when the local population is at a point of hopelessness and even desperation. The PLO, as an organization, remains for the Palestinians the only political institution that symbolizes Palestinian aspirations. The fact that support for the current PLO leadership falls to 71.2 percent against 93.5 percent support for the institution, shows, however, growing dissatisfaction with the concrete results accomplished by its leaders. The reason the Israeli public was so shocked by the poll is that for the Israeli, the status quo is peaceful with occasional periods of unrest, whereas for the Palestinian, the status quo is a war with periods of relative calm.

Political Developments

The period under review began and ended with hectic yet inconclusive efforts to convene an international peace conference. As in late 1985 and early 1986, the prime movers have been King Hussein of Jordan and the Israeli Prime Minister (later Foreign Minister) Shimon Peres. The same urgency that prompted them to embark on the abortive "Peace Initiative" of late 1985, carried them through 1986-87 in an almost desperate attempt to maintain a "momentum", based on multilateral negotiations, publicized "secret" meetings, and leaked rumours about "breakthroughs". Sharing, as they do, the perception that the Palestinian national movement, represented by the PLO, poses a fundamental and mutual threat to Israel and Jordan alike, they initiated and carried out a coordinated policy aimed at the destruction of PLO power bases both in Jordan and in the territories, and initiated a form of "power sharing" for controlling the Palestinian population. The abrogation in February 1986 of the Hussein-Arafat agreement of February 1985, and the closure (July 1986) of the PLO offices in Jordan, had paved the way for closer cooperation between Jordan and Israel.

The first step called for the replacement of Israeli officials, who, since 1982 administered West Bank cities, by local leaders, jointly appointed by Israel and Jordan. This was followed by negotiations on the reopening of the Cairo-Amman Bank in Nablus. Both steps were described by Israeli officials as part of a comprehensive plan of devolution and granting power to moderate Palestinian leaders. Negotiations were facilitated by active participation of U.S. officials, who regarded these steps as major achievements in implementing the policy of the "quality of life".

The first crimp in the otherwise relatively smooth relationship-building between Israel and Jordan occurred with the March 2, 1986 killing of Zafer al-Masri, the appointed mayor of Nablus by Rejection-Front assassins. The funeral turned into a mass demonstration in support of the PLO, against King Hussein's policies and Israeli Jordanian cooperation. All Arab mayoral candidates withdrew their names, and only six months later could Israel and Jordan complete the transfer of power to local mayors, and actually open the Nablus bank.

In an attempt to gain power and influence in the territories, Hussein pressured local PLO leaders and activists to shift their support to the crown and took actions against those who refused to do so. Pressure tactics designed to force PLO supporters to change loyalties took various forms. For example, Jordan closed its borders to PLO activists from the territories and did not allow others to leave Jordan for other Arab countries. PLO leaders were also arrested, interrogated, and had their passports confiscated when they crossed into Jordan.

All PLO supporters were dismissed from the Jerusalem Waqf, including its director. The president of a-Najah University was fired together with pro-PLO lecturers. Jordanian markets were closed to members of a Jenin agricultural cooperative who refused to sign a support announcement for Jordan. Passports have been issued by Jordanian clerks rather than local municipalities; and Jordanian clerks were appointed to administer development funds, so that the money would not fall into PLO hands. Village Leagues, organizations of the rural population once condemned by Jordan, were re-established with Hashemite funding.

In order to promote a positive image in the West Bank, Jordan created a propaganda machine which included a newspaper, radio and television programs. Due to al-Quds' cool reaction to the

King's February 1987 speech, Jordanian supporters on its staff resigned and helped establish an-Nahar, a new daily paper. Monetary support was also shifted from al-Quds to an-Nahar, which is often quoted in the Jordanian press. Radio and television programs aimed directly at the West Bank and Gaza populations stressed Jordanian-Palestinian "unity of fate", and included interviews with Palestinian personalities who expressed pro-Jordanian sentiments.

Jordanian measures were complemented by Israeli censorship of the Palestinian press' attacks against Hussein. The papers al-Mithaq, al-Ahad, al-Mawkef, and the offices of the Committee for Public Affairs were closed by the Israeli authorities. Israel deported Akram Haniyah, editor of the East Jerusalem newspaper, a-Sha'ab. Known for taking a pro-PLO, anti-Jordanian stand, Haniyeh was charged with being a senior Fatah organizer. All evidence against him was classified material to which he and his lawyers were denied access. This marked the first time in fourteen years that an editor was deported for publishing his opinions and not for specific subversive acts. It is also noteworthy that he expressed the opinions of mainstream PLO, which are shared by the majority of Palestinians, and not that of the Rejection Front.

In order to create economic bonds, or in other words, Palestinian economic dependency, as well as to create employment opportunities and a higher standard of living to prevent migration, Jordan announced a five year development plan for the West Bank and Gaza (see above). In promoting the plan, the Jordanians emphasized that most of the money will be used to develop the agricultural sector and rural areas to prevent Israeli settlement. In fact, Mount Hebron, a major power center of Jordanian support in the West bank, would receive the lion's share of the funds (see above).

According to the Development Plan, the agricultural sector will also benefit from the creation of a market, in Amman, that will sell West Bank produce throughout the Arab world. Jordan will also allow the importation of West Bank industrial products produced from raw materials imported through Israeli ports. Thus, exports will increase since materials will only be taxed upon entrance into Israel rather than at Aqaba port in Jordan and again at the Allenby bridge. This step was confirmed by the committee controlling the Arab League boycott, though it is still forbidden to export items made from Israeli natural resources or mechanization.

Physical planning schemes (see above) are carried out by Palestinian planners and financed jointly by the Civilian Administration and Jordan. Development projects in West Bank towns are coordinated by both countries, as well as export of agricultural products to Jordan. Jordan, with tacit Israeli blessing, has extended its financial support to Gaza Strip teachers, and helps finance projects in that region. Israeli officials solicited support in Western Europe for the Jordanian Five Year Plan.

Israeli spokesmen have attempted to elevate Jordanian-Israeli cooperation in the territories to the higher plane of "functional partition" or "interim arrangements". Shimon Peres, in the rare occasions when he referred to the substance of negotiations with Jordan under the umbrella of the "Peace Conference", mentioned "interim arrangements" of Jordanian-Israeli "power sharing", that would lead to "permanent arrangements" in the territories, and hinted that King Hussein has "agreed on principle to the scheme".

Observers differ on the motivation of King Hussein in pursuing his new West Bank policy. Some believe that he is still keen to regain the territory and is actively building a Hashemite power base there. Others, view his policy as preventive and defensive measures aimed at protecting his regime. The King, they maintain, is worried that radicalization and unrest in the territories would lead to major upheavals, including deportation of hundreds of Palestinian activists, which would spill-over instability to the East Bank. He is therefore compelled to pay the heavy political and financial price of maintaining the territorial status quo, and to facilitate the Israeli control system, in the hope that it will succeed in curbing the influence of PLO radicals.

The net result of Israeli-Jordanian cooperation is, that the status quo becomes more pervasive, and indeed, legitimizes a division of labor between the two countries to control the Palestinian population. It gives Israel a free hand in pursuing its policy of de-facto annexation of Israeli settlement enclaves, combined with shared-control with Jordan over the Palestinians.

It is ironic, that attempts to buttress the status quo are perceived as an integral part of the "peace process", and Jordanian-Israeli "Shared Rule" is not seen as a negation of the "peace for territories" equation on which the whole peace process is based. What cannot be denied, however, is that the "year of the last chance" for peace coincided with the intensification of the inter-communal strife in the territories. Reality refuses to comply with the perceptions of politicians.

FIVE: ISRAELI SETTLEMENTS

Demography

Demographic data on Jewish settlements on the West Bank are not collected in a systematic and objective fashion, and therefore are inaccurate. Furthermore, there are indications that data is inflated, for political and monetary purposes in order to demonstrate a strong momentum of settlement, and to justify demands for public assistance.

The main source of data is a bi-annual census, conducted by the Military Government. This census is ostensibly "restricted", but it is in fact widely circulated, and its figures are quoted by most observers, including the West Bank Data Base Project. An analysis of the census over time, however, casts serious doubts on its reliability. Inconsistencies, such as a decrease of 30 percent in the number of children (in a score of settlements) during one year; suspiciously rounded figures, grossly uneven composition of genders and other unexplained figures create the impression that reporting by settlers is far from being accurate.

Other sources, and especially government ministries that supply services to settlements quote different population figures. The Ministry of the Interior, for example, puts the number of settlers in the township of Emmanuel (1986) at 1,674, whereas according to the Military Government census it is 4,700. The population of Kiryat Arba is estimated by the Military Government at 4,440, whereas according to the Ministry of the Interior it amounts to 3,842 (1986). Figures of the Ministry of Education on pupils attending schools do not tally with those of the Military Government census. The lowest population figures of all, are used by the Central Bureau of Statistics (CBS). This source counts only settlers who changed their registration of domicile to West Bank settlements, a practice not followed by all.

The West Bank Data Base Project has tried to reconcile conflicting figures and to compile its own population estimates, relying on its long series of records, accumulated from all available sources. These estimates should, however, be treated with care and serve merely as indicators of general trends rather than as an accurate census.

As of April 1987 there were approximately 65,000 Jews, living in the West Bank, and some 2,700 in the Gaza Strip. Table 13 shows West Bank Jewish population growth in the last decade. The slowdown in the pace of settling, already noticed in our previous report, continued in 1986. The annual increase was 14.2 percent compared with 20 percent in 1985 and about 60 percent in 1984. Total increase in 1984-1986, however, was one third over 1984 figures.

As in 1985, almost the entire population increment is located in the urban settlements located in the metropolitan areas of Jerusalem and Tel Aviv. Map 9 and Tables 14 and 15 present total distribution of settlers by regions and absolute increment between 1984-1986. The concentration of settlers in the metropolitan area has reached 85 percent, compared to 80 percent in 1984. In fact, increment of settlers in metropolitan areas exceeded total increment due to decrease of settlers in the Jordan Valley.

The Jerusalem area is still the largest settlement area, mainly due to the rapid growth of Ma'aleh Adumim. However, the growth of the Tel-Aviv area is faster. Table 15 also shows that the average number of settlers per settlement in rural areas has decreased, and increased in the metropolitan areas.

The growth in the ideologically motivated settlements is slow even compared with the modest growth of 10 percent recorded between 1984-86 in the massif areas. An analysis of ten larger Gush Emunim settlements (Kedumim, Elon Moreh, Shiloh, Ofra, Bethel, Psagot, Alon Shvut, Kfar Etzion, Teqoa and Susia) show that total population growth in those settlements was 510 persons, including natural increase (9.3 percent) between 1984-1986. The crisis in Labor cooperative settlements in the Jordan Valley is apparent from the decrease of some 500 persons in that settlement area.

The third phase of the Israeli settlements process (following the initial Labor inspired Allon Plan and the Gush Emunim phase) is therefore well under way, and the suburbanization, or "yuppiezation" of the West Bank is gathering momentum. A recent unpublished report submitted to the Ministry of Housing provides a profile of suburban settlers in the Tel Aviv metropolitan area. More than 70 percent are under 30 years old, and are mostly young couples. The reported salary of one third is equivalent to the national average, while, 53.3 percent of the settlers earn more than the national wage average. Twenty percent are employed in the security forces (army, police); 25 percent in technical, engineering, and other white collar professions; and 29 percent are blue collar workers. Forty percent own private cars. Forty six percent are secular, 8 percent religious and the rest are "traditional". The average household size is 3.4 persons. Sixty one percent resided in the Tel Aviv area, especially in the eastern and north eastern towns of the outer ring. Sixty five percent indicated that the main reason for moving to the West Bank had been financial, 36 percent were attracted by the quality of life and pleasant surroundings. Sixty four percent considered buying an apartment within the green line, but found West Bank settlements less expensive and more attractive than the alternatives. Seventy five percent will not have to leave their present employment after moving to the West Bank settlements. Fifty five percent reported that they spent 30 minutes driving from their old home to work, and consider the additional 15 minutes, a "fair price" for their new home. They, however, would not consider buying an apartment 20 minutes further away (in the West Bank).

An earlier survey (conducted in 1983) indicated that there is a potential of 20-25,000 families residing in the Tel-Aviv metropolitan area, who were ready at the time to move to West Bank settlements, contiguous to the Tel Aviv area. Their motivation is non-ideological. Only 17 percent indicated Greater Israel ideological motivation. The rest indicated competitive cost of apartments, accessibility, and quality of life. The potential of settlers in the (West Bank) Jerusalem metropolitan area, is similarly, confined to young, predominately secular Jerusalem families. In 1985 not less than 8,000 Jerusalem residents moved to suburbs outside the municipal boundaries. The majority moved to West Bank settlements (Ma'aleh Adumim, Givat Ze'ev, Har-Hadar) but also to suburbs situated within the green line.

Present economic trends, growth of settler figures during the recession period of 1985 and part of 1986, the amount of building starts and stock of apartments, and the existing system of incentives (see below) brings us to the conclusion that at least until the mid-nineties market forces and "diffuse processes resulting from natural demand" would continue to operate and the average increase of settlements would maintain the 10,000 level annually. In the unlikely event of a major alteration in the incentive system there may be a change in demand patterns. However, as many suburban areas crossed the critical size-threshold (500-750 families), and infrastructure is completed, (schools, shopping centres, access roads) it would not seriously affect growth. The relative advantage of the West Bank metropolitan areas over alternative areas would remain high (proximity, relatively low land values, better climatic conditions, high standard of services). The security situation, and especially recurring incidents of deaths of commuters caused by fire-bomb and rock throwing, and vigilantes reprisals (see below), can have a serious effect on non-ideological settler demand. This has been the case in late 1986 and mid-1987.

All other things being equal, and barring unforeseen political and security changes, there is no reason to alter our 1982 forecast that, by the end of the eighties, settler population in the West Bank would reach 100,000 persons (excluding 120,000 in greater Jerusalem). The geographical distribution of settlers shows even greater concentration in areas closer to the green line, than anticipated by us in 1982. The areas affected mostly by Israeli settlement constitute approximately 20 percent of the total area of the West Bank and are inhabited by some 350,000 Palestinians (excluding 125,000 in greater Jerusalem).

The extremely limited growth potential of 70 semi-rural settlements of 4-6 years standing in the countryside is manifested by the fact that the average size of settlements (109 settlements, excluding 9 urban centers) remained almost unaltered since 1982. In 1982 there were 43.8 families per settlement. In 1983 – 46.5; 1984 – 47.4; 1985 – 47.4; 1986 – 48.8 families per settlement. In the semi-rural settlements incorporated in regional councils, 65 had less than 30 families and only 21 had more than 60 families in 1986. The same percentage (20 percent) of settlements with more than 60 families existed in 1984. The number of settlements with less than 20 families was 40 in 1984, and 38 in 1986.

TABLE 13

JEWISH POPULATION IN THE WEST BANK
(end of year)

	Total	Absolute increase	% increase
1976	3,176	–	–
1977	5,023	1,847	58.1
1978	7,361	2,338	46.5
1979	10,000	2,639	35.8
1980	12,424	2,424	24.2
1981	16,119	3,695	29.7
1982	21,000	4,881	30.3
1983	27,500	6,500	30.9
1984	44,146	16,646	60.5
1985	52,960	8,814	20.0
1986	60,500	7,540	14.2

Settlement Construction

During the years 1984-1987 (mid year), 11 settlements have been populated: 4 in Samaria (Migdalim, Oranit, Elkana C, Ganot Shomron); 2 in the Jordan rift valley (Beit Ha'arava and Maskiyot, formerly NAHAL outposts); 3 in the northern Judean hills (Nava, Hashmonaim, Har Adar); 2 in the southern Judean hills (Hadar Beitar, Karmei Zur). This, brought the total number of Israeli settlements on the West Bank to 118, compared to 109 in 1984. In addition, there were 16 NAHAL outposts. The World Zionist Organization blueprint for settling 100,000 Israelis in the West Bank (1983) called for the establishment of 164 settlements in the area by the end of 1986. Therefore, at the end of the target year, 80 percent of the settlement program has been implemented, but only 60 percent of its population target (see below).

Official sources claim that during 1984-1986 only three new settlements have been established. This assertion is based on the official definition of "settlements established", which, for the authorities, means "settlement in which work has commenced following a *new* government decision". Our settlement count is based on the population census, and we included all settlements in which settler presence has been reported during 1984-1986, and were empty (i.e. in various stages of construction) before.

TABLE 14

JEWISH SETTLERS BY REGIONS

Region	Absolute Number				Abs. Inc.	Inc. %	Average per Settl.		Percentages	
	1984	Settl.	1986 (June)	Settl.	1984-1986		1984	1986	1984	1986
Massif North	3,888	24	4,119	27	231	5.9	162	152	8.8	7.3
Massif South	972	15	1,217	16	245	25.2	65	76	2.2	2.2
Tel Aviv	13,895	20	20,212	24	6,317	45.5	694	842	31.5	35.4
Jerusalem(Q. Arba)	21,443	26	28,137	27	6,694	31.2	824	1,042	48.6	49.4
Jordan Valley	3,948	22	3,400	24	-548	-13.9	179	141	8.9	5.7
Total	44,146	107	57,085	118	12,939	29.3	—	—	100	100

The main settlement construction activity, however, occurred in existing settlements and specifically in the 10 urban centres incorporated as local councils (Emmanuel, Kiryat Arba – Hebron, Ma'aleh Adumim, Ephrat, Ma'aleh Ephraim, Alfei Menashe, Ariel, Elkana, Givat Ze'ev, Kokhav Yair), and in semi-rural settlements situated in Tel-Aviv (Western Samaria) and Jerusalem (Benyamin) areas.

Table 16 presents the various stages of apartment building activity. Out of 15,130 completed apartments 1,042 are vacant (6.9 percent); and 2,821 apartments are under construction. Therefore, the potential for settlement during 1987-88 comes, to 3,868 units. The Ministry of Housing has initiated a construction program of an additional 1,200 apartments, to be completed in 1989-90. The apartments under construction, are situated mainly in Western Samaria (55 percent), and the Jerusalem metropolitan area (31.3 percent). Table 17 shows that 56 percent of all apartments under construction are villas built under the "build your own home" scheme (see below), compared to 11.3 percent until 1984. Also, it reflects a government decision not to build prefabricated temporary apartments. The building stock will enable the authorities to maintain the pace of settlement of about 1,500-2,000 families each year. The increase of families settled between 1984-1986 has been 2,642.

TABLE 15

DISTRIBUTION BY METROPOLITAN AND RURAL AREAS

	1982	1984	1985	1986
Metropolitan areas	57.7	80.1	83.2	84.8
Rural areas	42.3	19.9	16.9	15.2
Total	100.0	100.0	100.0	100.0

Public Financing

Annual public investment in 1986 is estimated at NIS 210 million (US$140 million), excluding Ministry of Defense (military related) civilian investment. During 1985-86, US$350 million has been

TABLE 16

APARTMENTS IN WEST BANK SETTLEMENTS VACANT, OCCUPIED AND UNDER CONSTRUCTION BY TYPE OF SETTLEMENT 1986

	Occupied			Vacant			Under Construction			Occupied Apt. 1984/86			Total
Region	Semi-Rural	Urban	Total	Semi-Rural	Urban	Total	Semi-Rural	Urban	Total	Semi-Rural	Urban	Total	(1986) No Persor
Samaria	1,954	3,000	4,984	133	285	418	463	1,090	1,553	787	1,320	2,101	22,134
Benyamin	1,472	3,655	3,127	72	20	92	654	230	884	314	260	574	23,702
Etzion	682	264	946	85	–	85	85	56	141	33	64	97	5,151
Har Hebron	208	900	1,108	56	150	206	85	86	171	21	–	21	5,332
Jordan Valley	828	260	1,088	229	12	241	20	52	72	133	17	150	4,105
Total	5,144	8,109	13,253	575	467	1,042	1,307	1,514	2,821	1,288	1,661	2,949	60,424

Source: WZO

TABLE 17

APARTMENTS COMPLETED AND UNDER CONSTRUCTION BY TYPE

Type	Completed	Under construction 1987
Public Housing	11,653	1,235
Self-Built Villas	1,717	1,586
Temporary Prefabs	1,760	–
Total	15,130	2,821

invested, compared to US$520 million invested in the peak years 1984-1985. By 1987 the total Israeli capital outlay (excluding maintenance budgets, see below) since 1968 came to US$2.4 billion at current prices (see Table 18). At constant dollar prices this sum corresponds to approximately US$3.0 billion.

Public investment in West Bank settlements remained very high relative to other areas, and reached, in some sectors (industry, WZO, housing) 20-25 percent of total government development budgets. The official (Likud Government) settlement plan 1983-1986 (the "100,000 Settler Plan") envisioned total capital investment (from all sources) of US$2.5 billion in 4 years. US$375 million per year was planned to come from public budgets. Actual public investment during 1983-1986 came to US$870 million, instead of US$1,500 million or 58 percent of the planned outlay. Table 19 compares the "100,000 Settler Plan" objectives and actual data for the target year (1986).

Opponents of the settlement policy of the Likud would take comfort from the fact that the ambitious "100,000 Settler Plan" has not achieved its targets. They however, cannot ignore that during four years (1983-1986) the number of settlers has increased by 118 percent, housing units by 45 percent, and public investment by 56 percent. This considerable achievement is based on the continued priority given by Likud ministries to the settlement effort, which Labor ministers in the national coalition government were unable or unwilling to interfere with, except in rhetoric.

TABLE 18

INVESTMENT IN SETTLEMENTS 1968-1987

	Units			Investment in Mill. U.S.$				
	1982	1984	1986	1982	1984	1986	1986 %	Remarks
Housing Apartments	12,400	16,900	17,950	690	929	987	40.7	Including temporary, under const.
Industry production	1,260	1,610	2,362	328	418	614	25.4	Thousand sq. m.
Agriculture	55	55	55	55	75	95	3.9	Thousand dunams
Water	N/A	N/A	N/A	122	142	162	6.7	Main and local grids
Roads	200	–	288	75	90	101	4.2	Km. paved
Telecommunication	2,400	9,000	15,850	15	23	39	1.6	Subscribers
Electricity	N/A	N/A	N/A	15	25	30	1.3	Estimate excluding East Jerusalem elec. cor.
Education	N/A	336	432	–	40	51	2.1	Classrooms
Health clinics (ambulances)	N/A	71	98/61	N/A	4	7	0.3	Clinics/ambulances
Unspecified	N/A	N/A	N/A	250	325	335	13.8	WZO, transport community services, etc
Total	–	–	–	1,550	2,071	2,421	100	

– inapplicable
Source: WBDBP
Note: On methods of calculation see WBDB 1984 Report, p. 55-57.

TABLE 19

COMPARISON OF 1983-86 PLAN AND ACTUAL DATA

	Plan-1986	Reality-1986	% of Target
Settlements (No.)	164	130	80.0
Housing Units	33,360	17,950	54.0
Industry (dunams)	3,074	2,362	77.0
Agriculture (dunams)	100,000	55,000	55.0
Settlers	100,000	60,000	60.0
Roads (km)	595	288	48.0
Investment (public)	1,500	870	58.0

The priority given to the West Bank settlement is clearly manifested by comparing the incentives granted to settlers and entrepreneurs in the area, relative to development towns in Israel proper.

Less than 38 percent of development towns are granted the highest incentive status (A+) for industrial development (40 percent grant for the purchase of equipment, low taxation, subsidized infrastructure), whereas all settlement industrial parks are entitled to that status. Nineteen out of 29 development towns in the northern part of Israel (45 percent) and 3 out of 14 (22 percent) towns in the south are classified as "A+ towns". All 18 industrial settlements enjoy that status. Subsidy for housing (families lacking housing) in development towns, all in depressed areas, is NIS 26,000 (for families with up to 3 children) and NIS 38,900 in the West Bank. Families with 4-5 children receive 40,400 and 43,200 respectively; singles get 13,000 in development towns and NIS 19,500 in the West Bank. Settlers joining the "Build Your Own Home" scheme, pay for a state owned lot 16 percent of its assessed value in "A+" development towns (in Israel proper), 40 percent in "A" towns and 60 percent of its value in "B" towns. In all West Bank settlements one pays only 5 percent of the land value. Income tax reduction in development towns (only 18 of 35 towns are eligible) range between 3 – 10 percent. All West Bank settlements are eligible for 7 percent income tax relaxation.

The priority given to West Bank settlements assumes disproportional dimensions, when regular (maintenance) public allocations are analyzed. The average number of pupils in a West Bank settlement class is 26.3 (in local councils) and 25.6 (in regional councils). The Jewish educational system enjoys the highest possible standards ("enriched curriculum", extra curricular activities, etc.) which is expressed in higher average per-pupil expenditure. Yet, student bussing more than doubles education expenses. Out of NIS 10,460 million not less than NIS 6.4 million, are spent to transport 10,700 pupils and teachers within the region and to schools in Israel proper. The average annual expenditure on bussing Jewish regional councils' school children (in US$, 1987) was $688 per pupil. This ranged from $2,869 in Har Hebron council, $831 in Shomron, $816 in Mateh Benyamin, to $163 in compact Gush Etzion.

The major source for public expenditure remains the Ministry of Interior. This ministry is responsible for channelling government funds for financing the many services which local authorities provide. West Bank local authorities are considered an integral part of the Israeli local government system. The disproportionate allocations, reported by us in an earlier report (1986 report p.56) have decreased, on a per capita basis in 1986, due to an increase in the number of settlers and budgetary cut-backs. Per capita government grants-in-aid remained, however, 30-50 percent higher than per capita grants in similar local councils in Israel. Total government grants to local councils in the West Bank was US$14.7 million in 1984, US$13.2 million in 1986 and US$16.5 million in 1987.

Other government ministries (Religion, Defense, Health) provide an additional US$15 million, and the World Zionist Organization maintains absorption centers and Hebrew schools in settlements. The total regular (maintenance), state provided, budget is therefore estimated at US$45-50 million, and total public expenditure, at US$75-85 million.

Internal Development

Public financing of settlements (from all sources) is concentrated in the hands of regional councils bureaucracies, which allow them to amass considerable independence and economic strength. This power base serves them well in their political campaigning directed both at the government – pushing it to accelerate settlement construction, and at their political opponents who oppose settlement. Thus it enables them to launch independent settlement activities. The growing power of the settlers has worried the authorities, and especially Labor ministers in the national unity government. Their attempt to change the elaborate financial set-up that constantly broadens the settlers' power base has been frustrated by the organized settlers' lobby in the Knesset, consisting of scores of members. However, the settlers' clout is based on firmer ground. In ten short years they have succeeded in attaching themselves to those Israeli groups which enjoy preferential treatment, namely: "pioneering settlements", development towns and "confrontation settlements". That combined status made them eligible to receive subsidies and incentives and made them immune to being cut-off from public support. It is politically impossible to revoke their status, only to change the entire system of Israeli subsidies. The powerful pressure groups which rely on continued preferential treatment would not allow that, even if they are opposed to settlement in the West Bank. Thus, a Labor minister started a campaign against financial support to the settlers. When he realized that subsidies to "Labor settlements areas" (the Jordan Valley) as well as the kibbutzim are also involved, he dropped his initiative. Yet, it is the efficiency and organizational skills that settlers' leaders manifested, that enabled them to consolidate their power. They created a network of political and economic institutions, through which they are able to pursue their goals. In addition to the regional councils which combine political, financial, jurisdictional and planning powers, the settlers operate through three other institutions. These are "Development Corporations" (described in our 1986 report pp.58-59), 'Amana" and the Association of Israeli Settlers, YESHA).

Amana is the settlement movement of Gush Emunim. It was founded in 1976, when the Gush switched its priorities from protest activity to the establishment of settlements. It attained recognition as a "pioneering movement", by the World Zionist Organization and thus became equal to older and more venerable Zionist institutions such as the kibbutzim movement. Amana created a new form of settlement – the community settlement and community village, which unlike the older form of pioneering settlements have no agricultural characteristics or objectives. In

1987 there were 54 settlements incorporated in Amana, with an estimated population of 2,500 families. The disbursement of over US$200 million for the establishment and maintenance of these settlements enabled Amana leadership to achieve prominence in Gush Emunim at the expense of the traditional, ideological leadership. The preoccupation with pragmatic matters of budgets and physical development turned Amana leaders away from protest actions and vigilantes activities, a process which created a split in the Gush, between "pragmatists" and "radicals". The split came out into the open in May 1987, after the Gush secretary-general Daniella Weiss led a group of vigilantes on a rampage of rockthrowing and shooting in the town of Kalkilya after a fire bomb thrown on an Israeli car killed a Jewish woman. The pragmatists and moderates called for a change in the Gush leadership and its course of action. Yoel Bin Nur stated: "There's a difference between pushing for a certain policy constructively through building and progress, and a style of violence and intimidation". The radicals reacted by emphasizing the need for unity and by reminding the pragmatists that the "Gush had never been a movement that took the middle path and dealt with issues on which there has been a national consensus". The crisis was averted by a compromise but an angry exchange continues to fill many pages in the settlers organ, Nekuda.

The pragmatists find strong allies amongst the leadership of the non-ideological settlers with whom they participate in YESHA. The Association of Israeli Settlers was founded in 1979 and incorporates all settlements irrespective of their political and ideological affiliation. The activities of YESHA are financed by contribution of regional and local councils, taxes from settlers, contributions of government agencies and other public bodies. The executive arm of YESHA is composed of its chairman, the secretary general, and the heads of the regional and local councils in Judea, Samaria and Gaza.

YESHA had been initiated and founded by Gush Emunim activists, who are still controlling its activities. However, since 1984, when the population of the non-ideological urban settlers grew swiftly and outnumbered the ideologically motivated settlers, there has been growing tension between the two groups. The suburbanites objected to provocative actions of Gush vigilantes against the Arab population, and to agitation against Israeli military commanders who were blamed by the Gush for being "soft". The Yuppies also worried that heightened tension would affect the demand for West Bank apartments and scare off potential commuters. The relationship between security conditions and the flow of settlers was manifested in mid-1986 and again in April 1987, when sale of apartments in the West Bank Jewish townships almost ceased, due to violent incidents.

The heads of the non-ideological local councils are therefore supporting the Gush pragmatists in their effort to minimize confrontations with the Arab population and with the authorities. Their success is limited however. A growing number of settlers refuse to follow even the guidance of Gush radicals, and influenced by Rabbi Kahana's KACH hoodlums, they embark on murderous vendettas against defenseless Arabs, (Dehaishe Camp, June 1987).

CONCLUSION: THE SECOND REPUBLIC

In every discussion of subjects related to the West Bank and Gaza Strip – riots, settlements, demography, political initiatives – the mechanisms of suppression go into immediate action. Facts, data, processes, tools of analysis and control, scientific disciplines, sober situation assessments – all of these undergo a process of smelting and refining. The impurities – i.e. unpleasant facts – are thrown on to the garbage heap of prophecies of doom, while the refined material is placed in the mould of the prevailing "conception", and emerges in processed form: familiar, soothing and non-threatening.

Perceptions shape reality, not the reverse. Conceptual framework filters facts and data; cosy answers seeking facile questions.

Time has apparently stood still. Issues raised twenty years ago are perceived as perennially relevant, and are "solved" in the same way as they were "solved" in the past. Dilemmas defined a generation ago never seem to turn into problems requiring immediate decisions. All dangers are projected on to the distant future; all options remain open; all processes are reversible. Time is on our side (whoever we are). We are still right, good, sane and wise. Someone else is to blame: the PLO, the Zionists, the Left, the Likud, Gush Emunim, the U.S.A., the messenger bearing bad tidings. Compared to what the future could bring, the present is not so terrible.

We must therefore ignore the phantoms whispering that the future has already arrived, that we have passed the point of no return, that we have crossed the red line.

If not, we will have to act: change our image of ourselves, confront a disaster which has already taken place. We must construct ironclad scientific models to prove that options remain open and all prophets of doom (with their self-serving data and conclusions) are merely frustrated ideologues whose intention it is to spread despair.

In 1979 I published an article in which I wrote "the pattern created by Israeli policies and all social, economic, and political community interactions assumed a quasi-permanent nature ... the processes set in motion after 1967 are apparently so strong that integration has passed the point of no return". By 1983, after the Lebanon war I ventured to conclude that the clock had struck midnight and a new phase had begun. I wrote: "Theoretically, the process might be reversible, but a realistic estimate of the forces at work for annexation as against those that oppose it leads to the conclusion that for the foreseeable future all of Palestine will be ruled by an Israeli government; that the Israeli-Palestinian conflict has therefore become an internal ethnic conflict and that Israel is now a dual society".

My conclusions confounded my own wishes. They stood against everything I believed in. They amounted to an admission of total failure to prevent a situation I and my political friends warned against. Yet, I thought I should contend with the realities as I see them, and draw from the data, the conclusions that are closer to the truth as much as humanly possible.

I expected strong reactions but not the outpouring of abuse at my doorstep. This took the form of angry rebuttals and collections of essays distributed mainly by Israeli left- wing institutions. It took six years to construct alternative theoretical models that purport to demolish mine. The first model is Ian Lustick's "two threshold model of territorial state-building" (International Organizations 41,1, Winter 1987). Lustick distinguishes between three stages of "state building". The first is the "incumbency stage" in which disengagement from the territories means intense, but normal political bargaining and a decision to disengage depends on the ability to muster a parliamentary majority. The second stage, "regime stage" means that a proposal for disengagement raises extra legal challenges to the authority of state institutions, which threatens "regime integrity". In the third phase, the territories are universally perceived as an integral part of Israel, and are no longer an issue of debate. Attempts to secession "require raising fundamental questions about the community sense of itself and its rightful political domain". Lustick asserts that Israel is beyond the "regime threshold", meaning that the stability of the "Israeli regime" is indeed at stake, if disengagement should be proposed by an Israeli government. An Israeli government that suggests territorial compromise must therefore be prepared to risk "massive and violent challenge to its authority". Lustick argues, however, that the ideological or psychocultural threshold has not yet been crossed (except for East Jerusalem). Lustick's conclusion is that "the Israeli political system is prevented from serious attempts to withdraw ... because of threats to the stability of the legal order", but also because it is "too divided on the issue of treating the West Bank and Gaza as unquestionably permanent parts of the state." Therefore, while the process of annexation is at an advanced stage, it is still far from being "beyond the point of no return".

The second theoretical model is Sami Smooha's "continuous occupation" model (Politika, June 1987). According to him, the status of the territories is "unaltered after twenty years of occupation and the option of partition remains wide open". According to Smooha, it is the option of annexation that proved to be unrealistic and "the process of expanded 'Israeli state building' has encountered insurmountable difficulties". "Annexation has no chance", argues Smooha, "for the Jews are not ready to pay its full price – granting citizenship to Palestinians". The forces against annexation will remain strong and the international community will not tolerate it. According to Smooha the territories will therefore stay under occupation because the tests of annexation (official act of annexation, imposition of Israeli citizenship on the Palestinian inhabitants, considerable Jewish settlement, consensus of all Israeli political streams, recognition of the international community) will never be met. Smooha, therefore, criticizes Lustick who does not rule out annexation and is ready to admit that the process has progressed considerably.

The problem with both models is that they assume a linear progression from occupation to annexation (or full integration) and believe that annexation is indeed the objective of Israeli "territorial nation building" process. Until that fateful act of "annexation" takes place, the territories remain, according to Smooha, the way they were on the day military occupation was proclaimed, and all changes are either insignificant or reversible. Lustick recognizes some structural changes created during twenty years of occupation, but these changes have not affected, as yet, the "psychocultural" climate in Israel, except as far as Jerusalem is concerned.

Lustick ignores, of course, the fact that almost fifty percent of the West Bank (and not only East-Jerusalem) is beyond the "psychocultural threshold". "The future" of the Jordan Valley, Etzion Block, Greater Jerusalem, and its environs (Ramallah, Bethlehem) and Western Samaria is, indeed, "removed from the national political agenda", because "national consensus" (as represented by ninety percent of Knesset members and the political platforms of all major Israeli parties) exclude these areas from any territorial compromise scheme. The remaining territory, a long and narrow strip north and south of Jerusalem is considered by Labor "negotiable". An attempt to actually "disengage" from that area will, indeed threaten "regime integrity", but it is not likely to happen because the Arabs (even the Hashemites) are not likely to accept it as a starter. Therefore, such proposal of "disengagement" remains theoretical, and will not become a clear political choice.

The weakness of the theoretical models of "annexation" lies in the assumption that it will ever occur. The Israeli body-politic is precisely where it wants to stay. The present, fluid, amorphic situation is preferable and suits everybody. A better method than "annexation" has been found to integrate and segregate at the same time: to integrate the territories for Israeli interests (land, water, unlimited settlement, economic integration), and segregate the Palestinian population to avoid any burdens (citizenship, extension of Israeli welfare system, free political expression). Status quo usually changes when forces that seek to transform it are overwhelmingly stronger than the forces that wish to maintain it. In Israel, the power-relationship is in favor of the forces that view the status quo as the best of all worlds. Those who favor "annexation" do not need the formal act: one does not annex one's own homeland. The opponents of annexation are interested in perpetuating the occupation, because occupation indicate a *temporary* arrangement, which lead to still another illusion, that political options remain open and everything is fluid. Therefore one can believe that "nothing is irreversible". The theoretical end of the annexation process is therefore a fictitious point, and the "scale" – from "incumbency" to "ideological hegemony" is purely a theoretical construct. The present position of neither occupation nor annexation is probably the end of the process with some further refinements in the existing dual system.

"I can offer them no consolation", wrote Sigmund Freud, "for at bottom that is what they are all demanding, the wildest revolutionaries no less passionately than the most virtuous believers". Naked reality can offer us no consolation.

On the seventh day of the Six-Day war the Second Israeli Republic was established in the Land of Israel. Its political, societal, economic and administrative systems took form gradually, and are now consolidated, twenty years later.

Its government rules over all mandatory Palestine, and has the monopoly on governmental coercive power in the entire area under its dominion. The distinction between Israel's sovereign territory and the area in which it rules by military government has long since lost its meaning. It acts as sovereign, for all intents and purposes, in the whole of the area west of the Jordan river, changing the law as it wishes, and creating permanent facts.

The key to all legislation in the territories is the formulation: "anyone empowered to act in Israel according to Israeli law may so act in the territories". The Defense Ministry, through the Civil Administration, is, in effect, military governor of the "local" population, its jurisdiction being defined not as territorial, but ethnic. The Ministry of Housing decides how many flats will be built in Ariel and Kiryat Arba, in the same way as it decides how many apartments will be built in Petah Tikva.

All Israeli objectives have been attained in the territories and Jewish interests have been assured. The process of economic integration has long since been accomplished; infrastructure grids have been linked (roads, electricity, water, communications), administrative systems have been unified; social stratification has become institutionalized and political relationships have settled into well established patterns.

The Second Israeli Republic is a bi-national entity with a rigid, hierarchical social structure based on ethnicity. Three-and-a-half million Jewish Israelis hold total monopoly over governmental resources, control the economy, form the upper social stratum and determine the educational and national values and objectives of the republic.

The two million Palestinians divide into Israeli Palestinians and the Palestinians in the territories. Though the former are citizens of the republic, their citizenship does not assure them equality in law as one crucial test of citizenship is military service, and Israeli Palestinians who are exempt from service are, as a result, second class citizens.

The remaining one-and-a-half million Palestinians are citizens of a foreign state (in the West Bank) or stateless altogether (in Gaza). They are deprived of all political rights, ostensibly because they are under military occupation, though even their rights under international conventions governing military occupation are not assured, since the government of the republic does not recognize the application of these conventions to the territories.

The ethnic groups maintain economic interaction defined in professional literature as "internal colonialism", that is, the inferior ethnic group serves both as cheap labor and a market for finished consumer goods.

The Second Republic is, by any objective standard, a dual society and a political system whose technical term, again, in professional literature, is "Herrenvolk Democracy". The only reason this has not been universally acknowledged is that the territories have not been formally annexed.

Communal strife rages in the Second Israeli Republic. There is a perpetual conflict, not necessarily violent, between the Jewish majority group that seeks to maintain its superiority, and the Arab minority group that seeks to free itself from majority tyranny.

The majority community perceives the struggle as one of "law and order". The minority community, which does not regard the regime as legitimate, seeks to destroy it. Both communities deny each other's standing as a legitimate collective. Hence, the Arabs define Zionism (the expression of the collective aspirations of the Jewish people) as racism – ergo illegitimate. The Israelis, in their turn, define Palestinian nationalism as PLO terrorism – ergo illegitimate. The delegitimization is vital for both sides, for it enables them to believe in the exclusivity of their claim and in the absolute justice of their position.

Both communities, though internally divided, outwardly present a monolithic facade. The Israeli consensus comprising the vast majority of the Jewish group is united in its aspiration to preserve the Jewish character of the Second Republic, i.e. its superior status, even at the cost of democratic values. While the differences between the main Jewish political factions are those of emphasis, style and abstract moral scruples, even these vanish utterly on the daily, tactical level. The vast majority of the Arab group is united in the desire to destroy Jewish hegemony, and is divided only over the most effective method of achieving their objective armed struggle or "sumud", steadfastness. Just as all Israelis are Zionists, so too, are all Arabs PLO.

The dynamic of the Israeli Palestinian communal strife is similar to that of intercommunal conflicts everywhere – from Beirut to Belfast. It is waged in an endless cycle of violence, enforcement, domination, containment – fights over every piece of land, every tree. It is accompanied by the development of stereotypes, a lowering of the threshold of moral sensitivity, the loss of humanistic values, and despair leading ultimately to psychological withdrawal, to anarchy and fundamentalism.

The carrot-and-stick method which, in the absence of long term policy is the inevitable means of control, only exacerbates the conflict. The rise in the standard of living of the subject population sharpens its feelings of frustration and outrage. Exposure to the open society hastens the modernization process of the minority and the sophistication of its political struggle. The conflict erupts periodically, usually following an unplanned provocation, and quickly dies down. Violence simmers just below the surface. It is an endemic condition, lacking a durable solution.

The actual existence of the Second Israeli Republic is not in danger. The grim forecasts of disintegration of the republic from within, as a result of communal strife, demographic balance or Arab resistance are implausible. The balance of power between the Jewish and Arab communities is decisively in favor of the Jews, and the gap is widening. The resources at the disposal of the government and the sophistication of its system of enforcement, ensure that any attempt to threaten the system will be crushed. The strength of the system is based on the cohesiveness of the Jewish consensus and its readiness to support the regime. Such support is guaranteed because the political center perceives the conflict in term of survival. Terrorist activity and protest by the minority sharpen the feeling that there is no real alternative and act to strengthen belief in the justice of the cause.

The almost axiomatic conviction that the Israeli-Arab conflict is the core trouble of the region remains an ideological precept, but has long been overtaken by events. The perception that the fertile crescent is still in the era of wars whose outcome could change the geo-political map is the premise prompting diplomats and politicians to engage in a "peace process". Yet, this premise is in itself obsolete after Camp David, the Israeli-Egyptian peace treaty, and the Lebanon campaign of 1982.

These events ushered in a new phase for Israel and its neighbors that can be termed *unstable equilibrium*. It is an unstable system maintained by Israel and Syria, each for its own purposes. Both sides need the conflict to continue unresolved, but in a manner that will not explode into an all-out war. This equilibrium is facilitated by the cold, yet durable peace between Israel and Egypt, the vulnerability of the Hashemite regime in Jordan, and the profound impact of the Iran-Iraq war. The notion that the Palestinian cause can serve as a battle-cry that will shatter this unstable equilibrium is maintained only by a minority of ideologically motivated observers in Israel and in the West, who in their despair believe in a *deus ex machina* capable of resolving the century old, Jewish Arab feud.

The Palestinians themselves have given up hope for their brethren. The Arab states care very little about the Palestinians, as was clearly demonstrated during the Lebanon campaign and thereafter. They believe they have done what they can for the Palestinians and they maintain involvement in the Palestinian cause only when it serves their interests.

The Israeli-Arab conflict, which for 40 years has been a region-wide, inter-state conflict, has shrunk to its original core, namely *Israeli-Palestinian intercommunal strife*. This major turning point, which, if true, renders the traditional paradigm obsolete, and requires reformulation of options and choices, is not acknowledged by most observers.

To understand the new phase in Israeli-Palestinian relationship one must return to the formative phase of this tragic encounter. To be sure, one could fix the starting point at the end of World War I, or even earlier, in 1882, when the first Zionist settlement was established. But the mid-thirties, and more specifically, the Arab

Revolt of 1936 and its aftermath – more accurately define the contours of the dispute, and form the point to which we can trace back present relationships, perceptions and strategies.

By the mid-thirties, both the Jewish and the Palestinian communities had developed into cohesive and self sustaining societies, and moved irrevocably and consciously toward total confrontation. The Palestinians, aware of their growing national power, endorsed the "armed struggle" as their strategy, and launched the Arab Revolt – a mighty effort to overthrow the British Mandate, and destroy the Zionist enterprise. Their primary target was the British, because they viewed the Zionists as white settler colonists, totally dependent on the British, a non-viable society bound to disappear once the colonial power was ousted.

The Zionist reaction to that mortal danger was equally powerful. Even the most moderate among them understood that a bloody showdown was inevitable. They had to abandon their earlier, naive and self-serving perception of the conflict as an international class struggle, or as a tragic misunderstanding caused by the ignorance of the natives who could, in time, learn to accept the Jews because of the material benefits they brought. The Zionists realized that they were facing a national movement, but could not grant it legitimacy; they therefore depicted it as a fascist, reactionary gang of murderers. The Zionists, like their adversaries, viewed the Palestinians as a nonviable society, an offshoot of the Arab world, not as an independent factor.

Since 1936, the perceptions of both Palestinians and Jews have been characterized by exclusionary attitudes, and the conflict is perceived as a zero sum game and an externally generated dispute. Both sides either ignored or underestimated the other side, viewing it as an object, manipulated by external forces. As a result, they saw no point in trying to relate to their adversary directly.

The defeat of the Palestinians in 1937-38 prompted the neighbouring Arab countries to take over their cause, which only served to confirm Jewish perceptions of the Palestinians as an externally generated force. The 1948 war reinforced these perceptions. The total collapse and destruction of Palestinian society completed the process of externalization, as objective reality caught up with perceived reality. Intercommunal strife became a conflict between sovereign states. It became the

Israeli-Arab conflict. The Palestinians themselves assisted the Israelis in redefining the conflict. During the pan-Arab, Naserite era, Palestinian activists perceived their national struggle in a broader, anti-imperialist context. They clung to their old perceptions viewing the "Zionist entity" as a neo-colonial, non-viable phenomenon, relying for sheer survival on the imperialist power.

The 1967 war, the occupation of the West Bank and Gaza, and the 1973 war, have not changed these perceptions which by now have become a fundamental credo. They persist even after the signing of the Israel-Egyptian peace treaty. They have not changed despite rising inter-communal strife between Jews and Arabs in the occupied territories, for they satisfy deep-seated psychological needs, and enable both sides to believe in the exclusivity of their claims.

The inability of either side to accept the legitimacy of the other as an enemy, let alone a partner for peace negotiations, is central to the understanding of the failure of traditional diplomacy in its attempt to resolve the Israeli-Palestinian dispute. Intercommunal disputes of such proportions are beyond diplomacy. Hence, attempts to resolve it through a conventional "peace process" approach are bound to fail. In order for the peace process to be effective, certain conditions must be met. First, it must take place within the context of an international system.

The basic right of the enemy to a legitimate, autonomous identity is not itself in dispute; rather it constitutes the premise on which negotiations are possible to begin with. It is only within this procedural context that the peace process can function. The peace process must proceed on the assumption that the conflict is not a zero sum game, and the belligerents must be prepared to participate in negotiations in which concessions and compromises can take place; issues must be translatable into clearly defined choices.

Only because all those conditions were met, was the peace process between Israel and Egypt successfully concluded. It is because none of these conditions can be met, that the Israel-Palestinian dispute cannot be resolved through a similar process.

In Security Resolution 338, both Israel and Egypt agreed on a means end effort to transform belligerency into peace relations, within the context of the international system. Sadat's visit to Jerusalem symbolized the recognition of Israel as a legitimate actor and the Israeli public as an autonomous and independent constituency. Secret Israeli-Egyptian meetings (prior to official negotiations) established a positive sum game: the return of Sinai and an unconditional recognition of Egyptian sovereignty in exchange for security arrangements. Disputed issues could be reduced to concrete items on which concessions and compromises were possible.

The Israeli-Palestinian dispute is bogged down in the critical pre-procedural phase. Although objective observers like to define the dispute as a clash of national entities struggling for the same land, this definition is not shared by the adversaries. The core of this conflict is understood by them as "survival". The struggle goes beyond the psycho-sociological survival of the parties involved, to basic issues of identity and integrity.

The core of the dispute is non-negotiable, for issues of identity are a zero sum game. Neither side can afford to take the risk of recognizing the other as legitimate, for it would jeopardize its own claim. For the Israelis, mere recognition of the Palestinian claim would negate their own legitimacy and existence. For the Palestinians, recognition of the Israelis means a fatal dilution of their claims and a surrender of their trump card.

We pointed out that the peace process must take place within the framework of the international system. In order for this to happen, both parties must be full members of that system. Negotiations must take place around tables with representatives of the belligerent parties equipped with their symbols of legitimacy – diplomatic credentials, flags and national anthems.

But the very heart of the conflict involves the legitimacy of these symbols. Participation itself implies a symbolic concession too great for the opposition. In the normal peace process, enemies recognize the other's legitimacy to exist as an entity, albeit, a belligerent one. In the Palestinian-Israeli conflict that very existence is in dispute.

To be sure, the status of Israelis and Palestinians is asymmetrical. Israel is recognized as a sovereign state, and her legitimacy is not disputed by most countries (including some Arab countries). The Palestinians are internationally recognized as a quasi-national entity, but that status is too ambiguous to allow them participation in the international system as equal partners. Full recognition is denied them, because independent, equal status implies acknowledgement of their right to self-determination and the existence of an autonomous and separate constituency represented by a recognized leadership. This denial of basic recognition of the Palestinians is shared by the three principal actors in the process, namely, the U.S., Jordan and Israel. The Palestinians, for their part, refuse to recognize Israel. It is basically Israel's veto and Palestinian refusal, that prevent any progress.

Yet, the process must continue. So, palliatives are concocted to bypass the stumbling block. An artificial constituency, Jordanian-Palestinian, is invented to externalize the Palestinians, and attach them to a "legitimate" collective. Alternative, "authentic" Palestinian leadership is sought, an international umbrella is devised to circumvent the mutual recognition issue. U.S.-Palestinian overtures are pursued as a form of indirect pressure on the Israelis. All these attempts fail, for the core problem cannot be tackled. "Peace initiatives", critical to the peace process jargon, repeatedly fail, because the Israel-Palestinian conflict cannot be squeezed into that jargon.

The adversaries themselves perceive their conflict in a different context, that of inter-communal strife. It is fought by young Palestinians born into the occupation, by Jewish zealots who believe in divine guidance, by young Israeli conscripts shooting Palestinian youth because they are told they are fighting for survival, by terrorists planting bombs in civilian airplanes.

The diplomatic process can provide no remedy for the intercommunal strife, so it seeks to contain it, and to stabilize the status quo while retaining the rhetoric of the peace process. The powers directly involved in the diplomatic process, the U.S., Jordan and Israel, are well aware of the inherent contradiction between the preservation of the status quo of Israeli occupation, and a peace process based on peace-for-land formula. They do, however, worry that the exacerbation of intercommunal strife could threaten the unstable inter-state equilibrium. This could occur if internal Israeli-Palestinian tension becomes unbearable through acts of terrorism and Israeli retaliation and encroachment. Israeli extremists might then seek to transform the status quo by making Ariel Sharon or his successor Prime Minister of Israel. He will see to it that enough Palestinian activitsts will be deported. Then, with a tacit agreement with Syria destabilize the Hashetmite regime, thereby creating Palestine in Jordan. Then, the West Bank will be transformed into an oriental Alsace-Lorraine. The Jordan will be the Rhine of the Middle East and a situation similar to that which prevailed between Germany and France in the 18th century would evolve. To counter such an eventuality, efforts are made to stabilize internal conditions through economic aid, and other micro-arrangements.

That policy of pacification – mistakenly perceived as identical with the peace process – may, in the short run succeed. The parties directly involved are capable of maintaining it through a judicious combination of carrot-and-stick methods. Ironically enough, the Palestinains, against whom this policy of containment and pacification is aimed, are themselves contributing to the preservation of the status quo. Their negativist, indeed, self-destructive policies allow no option other than maintaining the status quo, which seems better than any alternative. The status quo is, thereby, not only reinforced but also legitimized. As a result, the peace-for-land equation loses its relevance, and the peace process loses its meaning.

To minimize this inherent contradiction, an attempt is made to depict the status quo as a static situation, frozen at a stage which leaves all options open. Basic data and facts are ignored or misinterpreted. Decisions on micro-issues such as the opening of a bank or the appointment of an official, are made during secret meetings of diplomats. This contributes to maintaining the illusion of a peace process and the fiction of momentum. Improvement of economic conditions as an instrument of political change (a Marxist concept, curiously used by conservative-capitalist countries), assumes top priority.

Yet, the attempt at self-deception cannot affect reality and is not even shared by those involved. They understand the policy in the context of the struggle in which they are engaged. The Israelis interpret it as license to pursue their policies of annexation; the Palestinians – as attempts to bribe and fragment them. The net result is that intercommunal tensions are exacerbated. The leverage applied is too flimsy to pull the vehicle out of the mud; the inevitable outcome is that it sinks even deeper.

Twenty years of Israeli domination have created a powerful process of Palestinian nation building. Ironically, it could have taken place only under Israeli occupation because it presented a powerful challenge, a real threat, to the cohesion of Palestinian society and to Palestinian national identity.

The response was equally powerful. The improvement of the standard of living, proletarianization of the peasantry and urbanization produced social mobility. A tremendous thirst for education and investment in human capital began. Social and political awareness have grown. Voluntary, autonomous community networks and institutions have developed to counter Israeli attempts at the fragmentation of Palestinian society.

The occupation has produced the seeming paradox of a helpless yet vibrant community. Young Palestinians who were born into the occupation are less ready to accept the status quo, and manifest stronger resistance to the occupation. This process should not be perceived as identical with support of the PLO as an effective political institution. The overwhelming majority of Palestinians certainly support the PLO as a symbol of Palestinian nationalism, but there is growing disillusionment with the notion that the PLO can act effectively to deliver them from their predicament.

Palestinians under Israeli domination are unable to formulate a constructive political strategy. The total ban on regional political activity and harassment and deportation of Palestinian leaders seriously hinders public political discourse. From the other side, threats of reprisals, intimidation and assassination of Palestinians who dare express views divergent from official PLO positions, discourage all but a very few.

The main obstacle is, however, more basic. Under most optimistic assessments, the Palestinians will manage to hold their ground in the territories. This is no solution for more than two million Palestinian expatriates whose aspirations are expressed in a fundamental credo of the PLO *al-awda* (the return) to Jaffa and Acre.

Formulating a realistic strategy means that those Palestinians must be told to give up that hope. No local Palestinian leader is courageous enough to tell his displaced brothers this objective truth. They would treat him as a traitor to the cause, and rightly so from their point of view. A Palestinian leader must be capable of challenging the status quo, while recognizing the objective constraints which cannot realistically be changed. Such a gradual, constructivist approach will be viewed as defeatist and even treasonable.

Because no such challenge is presented to the Israelis, they continue to see themselves engaged in a struggle for survival and to believe in the justice of their position vis-a-vis the Palestinians. Most see no alternative to the status quo of occupation. It does not nag their conscience, because the dual system of superiors and inferiors is perceived as politically necessary for security reasons. They are not forced to choose between patriotic and liberal-democratic values. Faced with Palestinian negativism, all alternatives to total control seem unacceptable.

The concept of an internally generated, endemic civil war ought to replace the outmoded view of the Israel-Arab conflict as an inter-state externally generated dispute. While the international community can play a role in containing the dispute so that it does not spill over and threaten international stability, external forces cannot replace the communities engaged in the struggle. They must themselves realize that continued strife will bring a plague on both their houses, that nobody emerges triumphant from a communal strife and one community cannot thrive forever on the misery of another.

LIST OF SOURCES

CBS, *Statistical Abstract of Israel*, No. 37, 1986

- Reported live births for Judea, Samaria and the Gaza Area up to 1984, *Judea, Samaria and the Gaza Area Statistics*, No. 1, 1987.

- Population Estimates for Judea, Samaria and Gaza Strip up to 1984, *Judea, Samaria and the Gaza Area Statistics*, No. 1, 1987.

- *Projections of Population in Judea, Samaria and the Gaza Area up to 2002*, Special Series no. 802, Jerusalem 1987.

- *Judea, Samaria and the Gaza Area Statistics*, No. 2, 1987

Ministry of Health, *Health and Health Services in Judea, Samaria and Gaza Area 1985-86*, Jerusalem 1986.

Bahiri, S., *Industrialization in the West Bank and Gaza,* West Bank Data Base Project and the Jerusalem Post, 1987

Dehter, A., *How Expensive Are West Bank Settlements,* West Bank Data Base Project and the Jerusalem Post, 1987

Kahan, D., *Growth and Stagnation: Agricultural Development in the West Bank and the Gaza Strip*, West Bank Data Base Project and the Jerusalem Post, 1987

Israeli Knesset, *Government Budget Books*, 1986/7, 1987/8.

Kingdom of Jordan, *A Programme for Economic and Social Development in the Occupied Territories 1986-1990: Profile of the Development Projects, Amman, October 1986: Summary*, November, 1986.

Civilian Administration: *Judea and Samaria, Regional and Local Councils, Enactments and Regulations*, September, 1986.

WZO, Judea and Samaria: *Report on Status of Development, 1986*, Jerusalem, 1987.

West Bank Data Base Project, *Computerized Abstract of Newspapers 1986-1987.*

MAPS

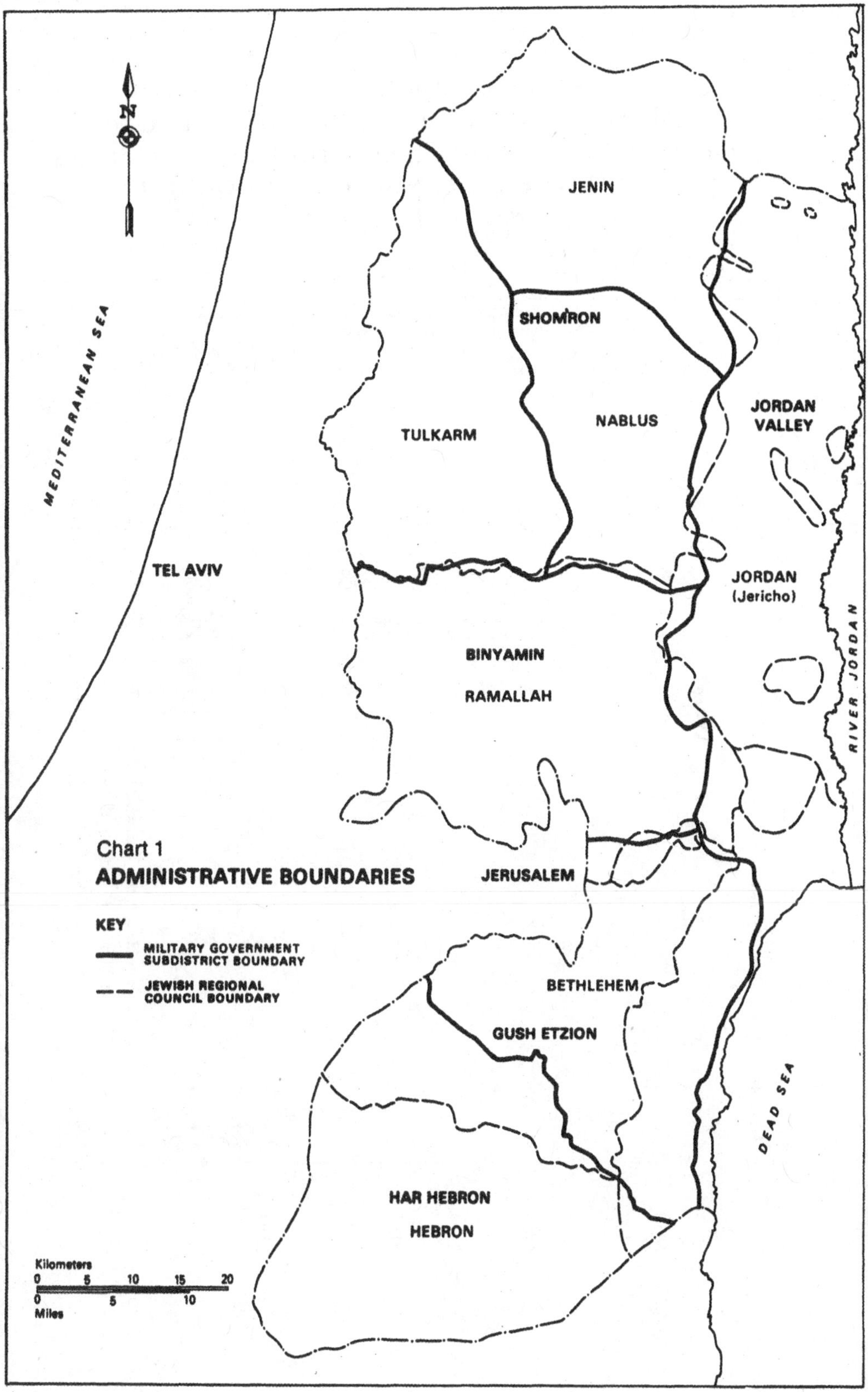

Chart 1
ADMINISTRATIVE BOUNDARIES

KEY

MILITARY GOVERNMENT SUBDISTRICT BOUNDARY

JEWISH REGIONAL COUNCIL BOUNDARY

Chart 2

COMPARISON OF ANNUAL EXPENDITURES ON COMMUNITY SERVICES IN SELECTED NEW SETTLEMENTS OF MATEH BENYAMIN REGIONAL COUNCIL

(in U.S.$ per family)

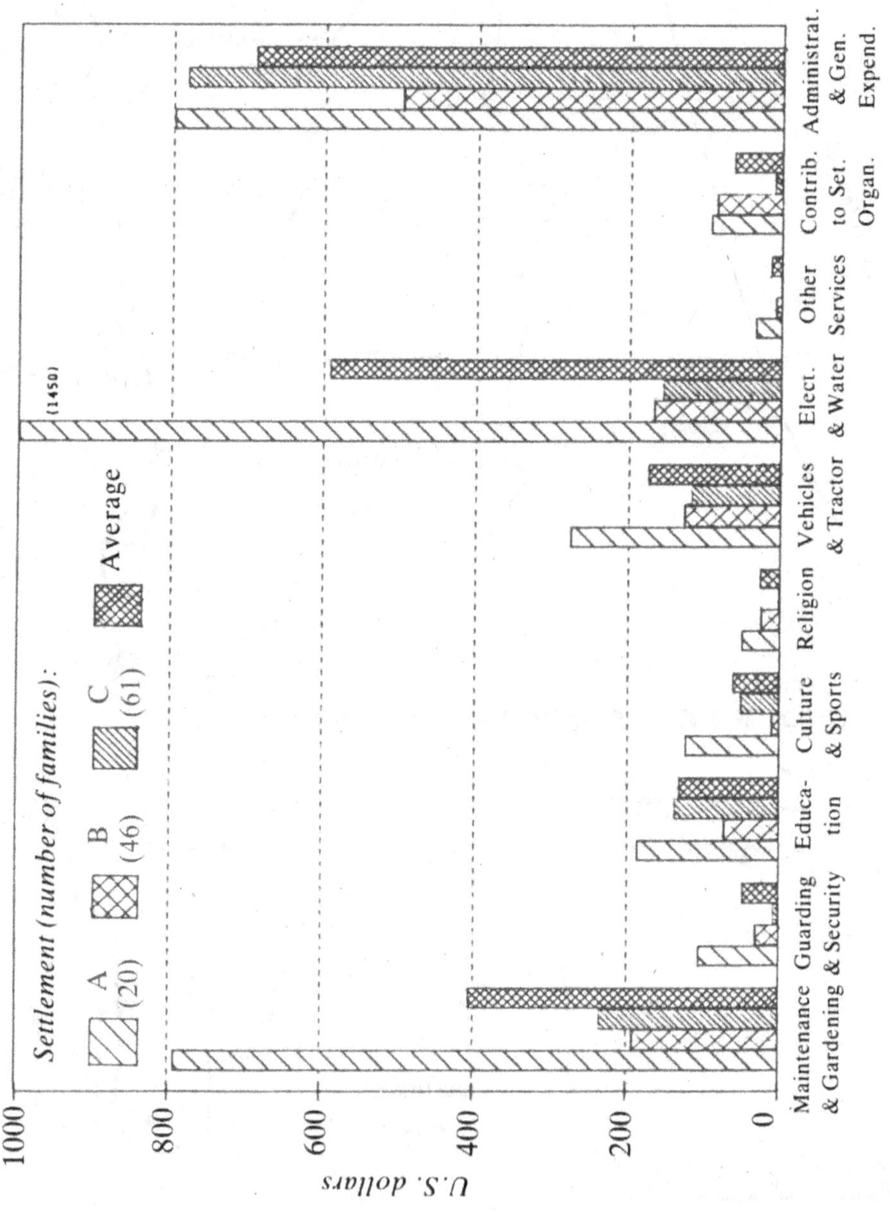

Chart 3
AVERAGE EXPENDITURES ON SOCIAL SERVICES IN ALL REGIONAL COUNCILS IN THE WEST BANK AND IN ISRAEL
Ordinary Budget 1983-84

(in U.S.$ per capita)

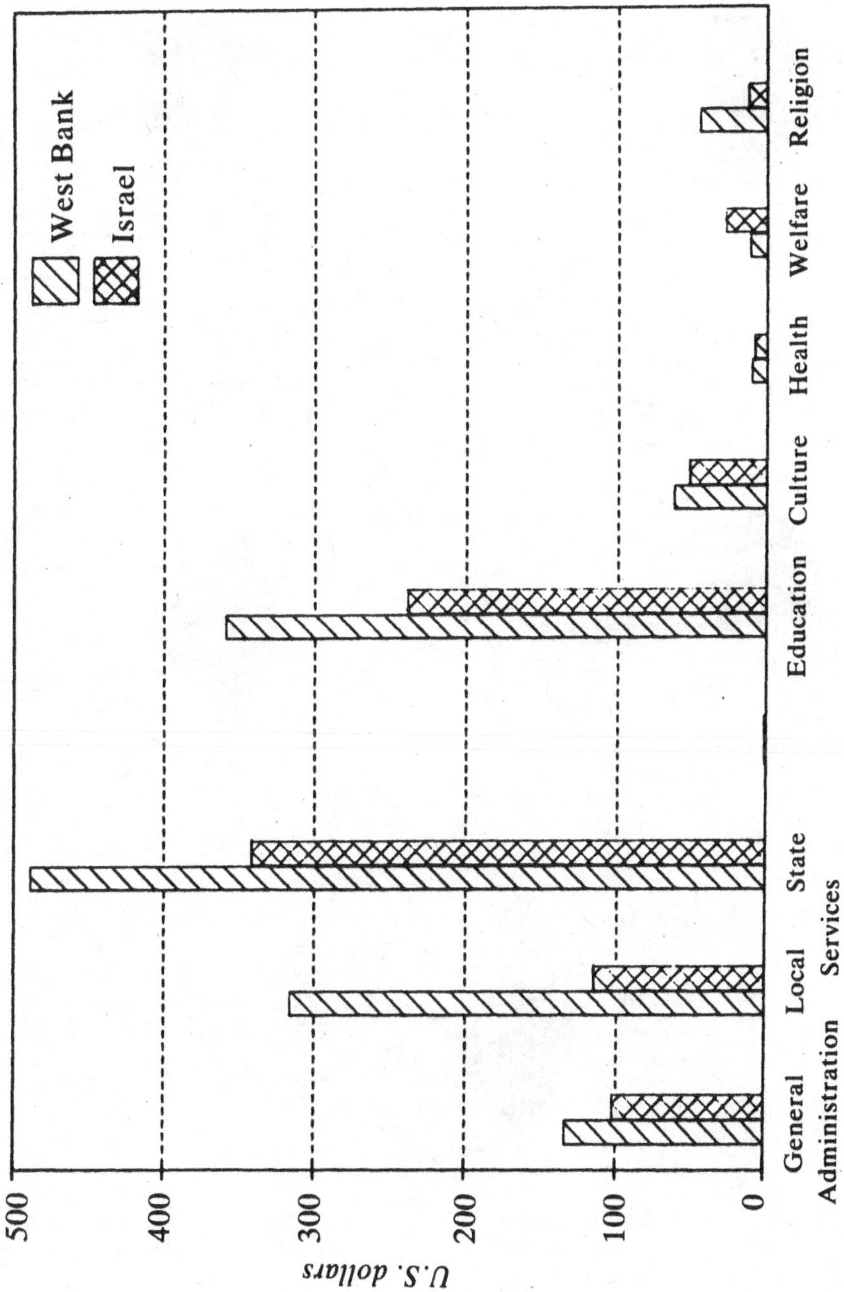

Chart 4

COMPARISON OF AVERAGE REVENUE SOURCES FOR PROVISION OF SOCIAL SERVICES IN ALL SMALL LOCAL COUNCILS AND ALL REGIONAL COUNCILS IN THE WEST BANK AND IN ISRAEL (Ordinary Budget 1983-84)

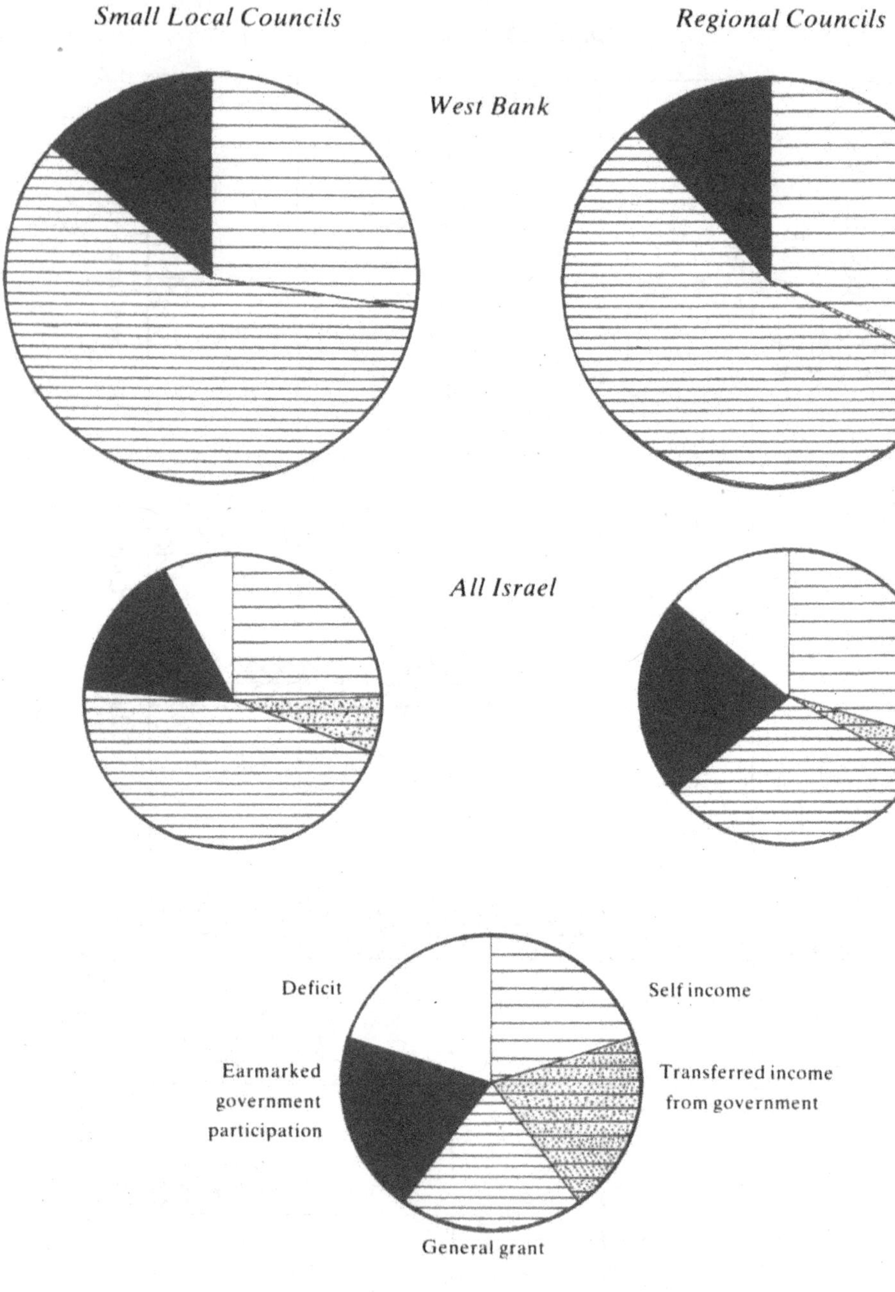

Chart 5
AVERAGE REVENUE SOURCES FOR PROVISION OF COMMUNITY SERVICES IN NEW SETTLEMENTS OF SELECTED REGIONAL COUNCILS

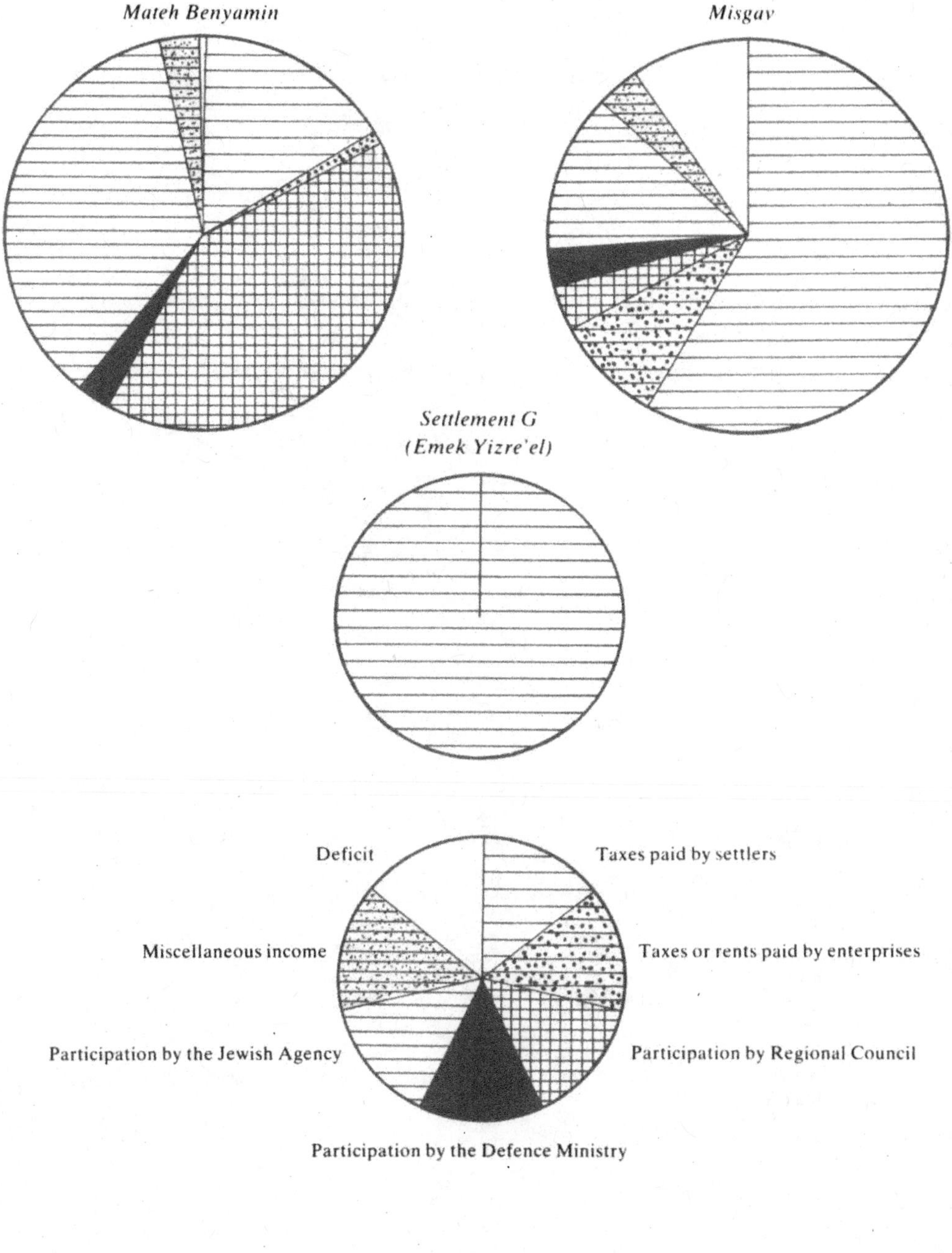

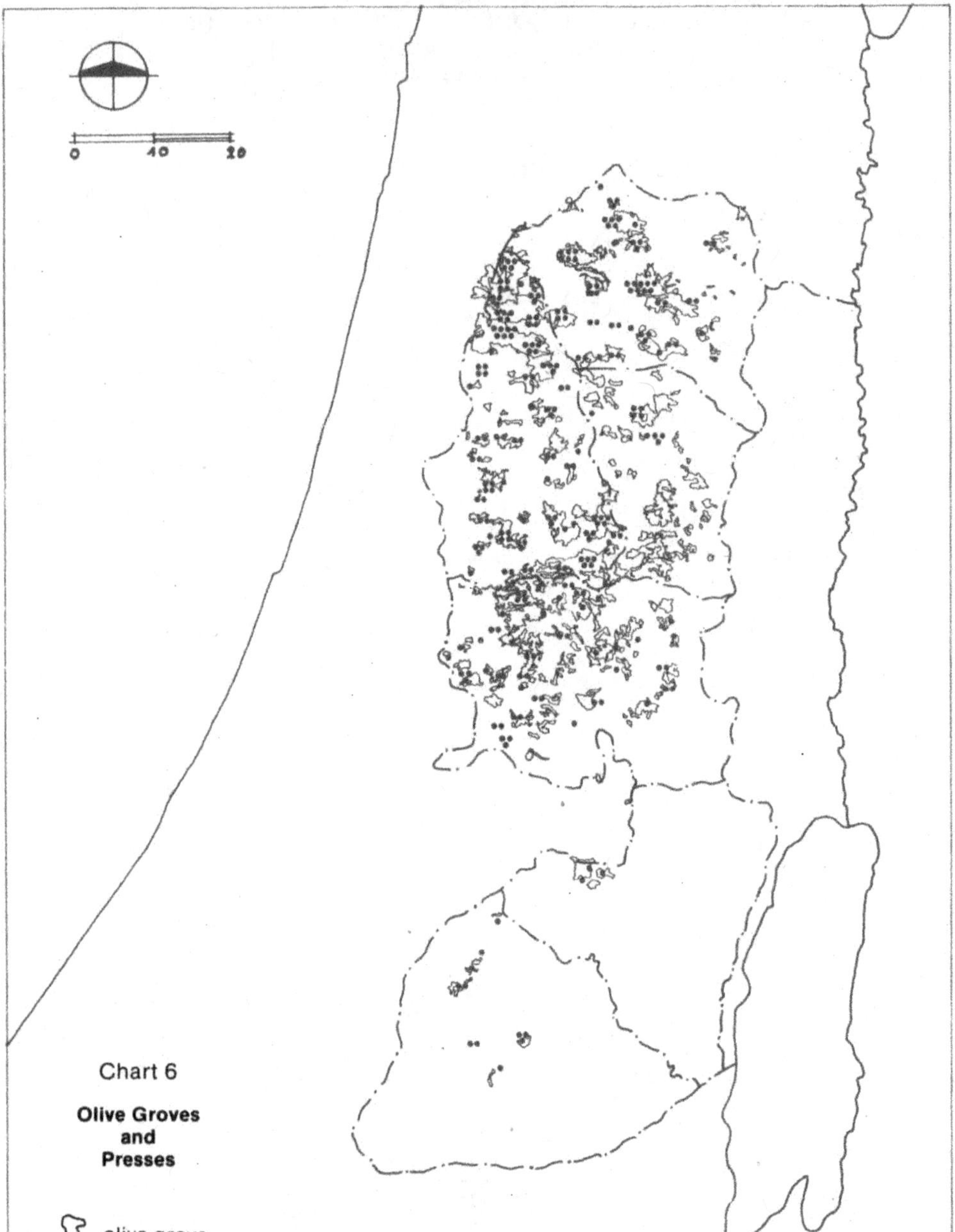

Chart 6

Olive Groves and Presses

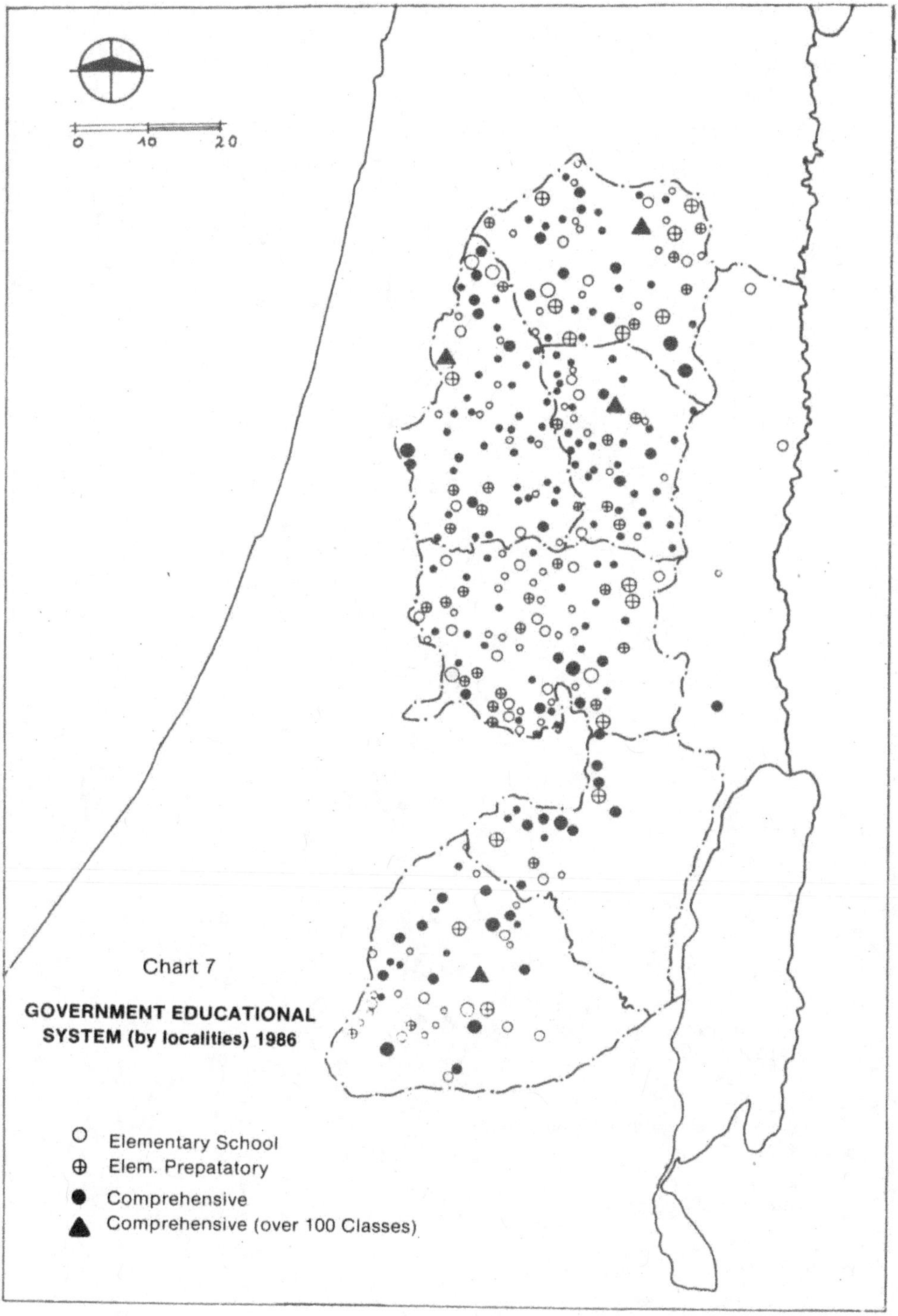

Chart 7

GOVERNMENT EDUCATIONAL SYSTEM (by localities) 1986

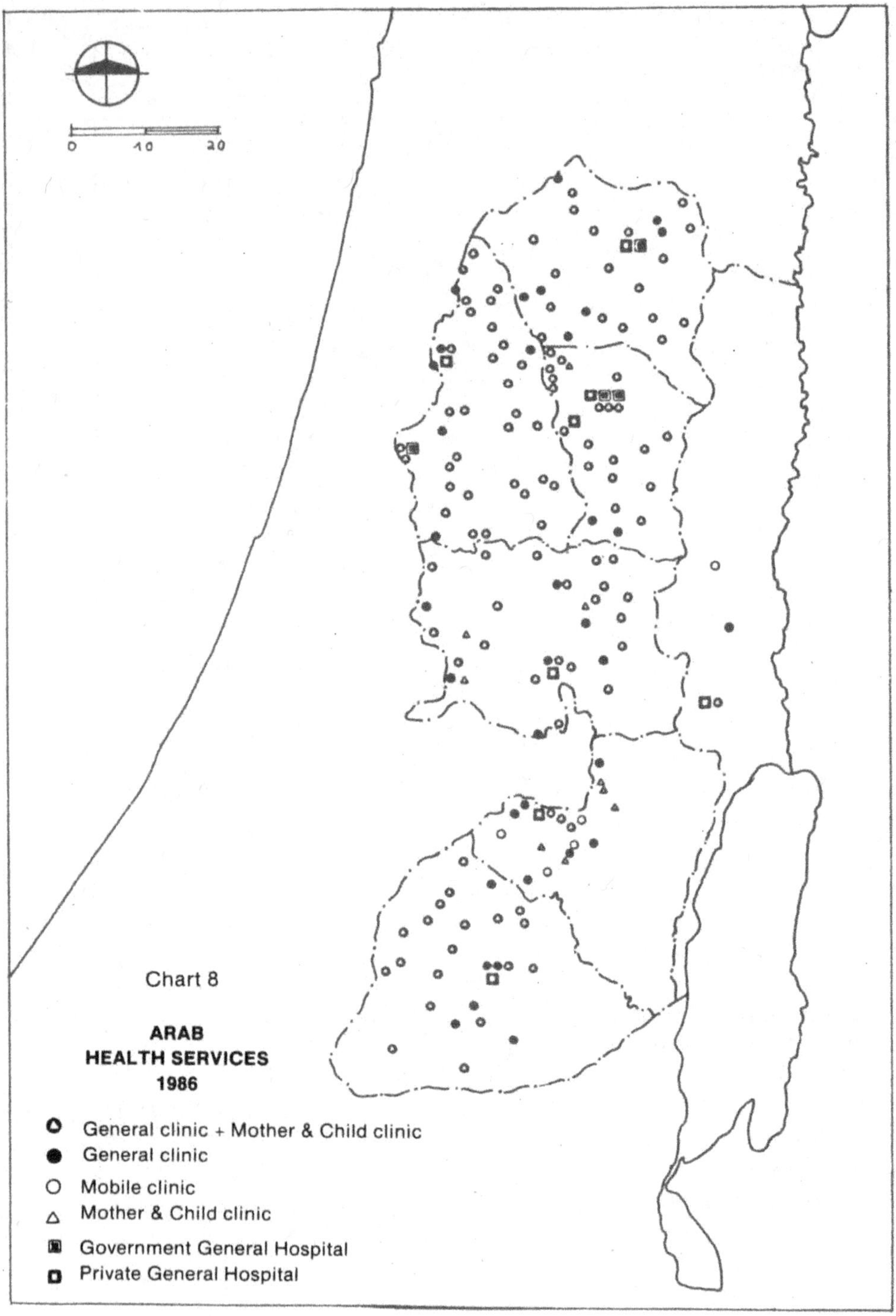

Chart 8

ARAB HEALTH SERVICES 1986

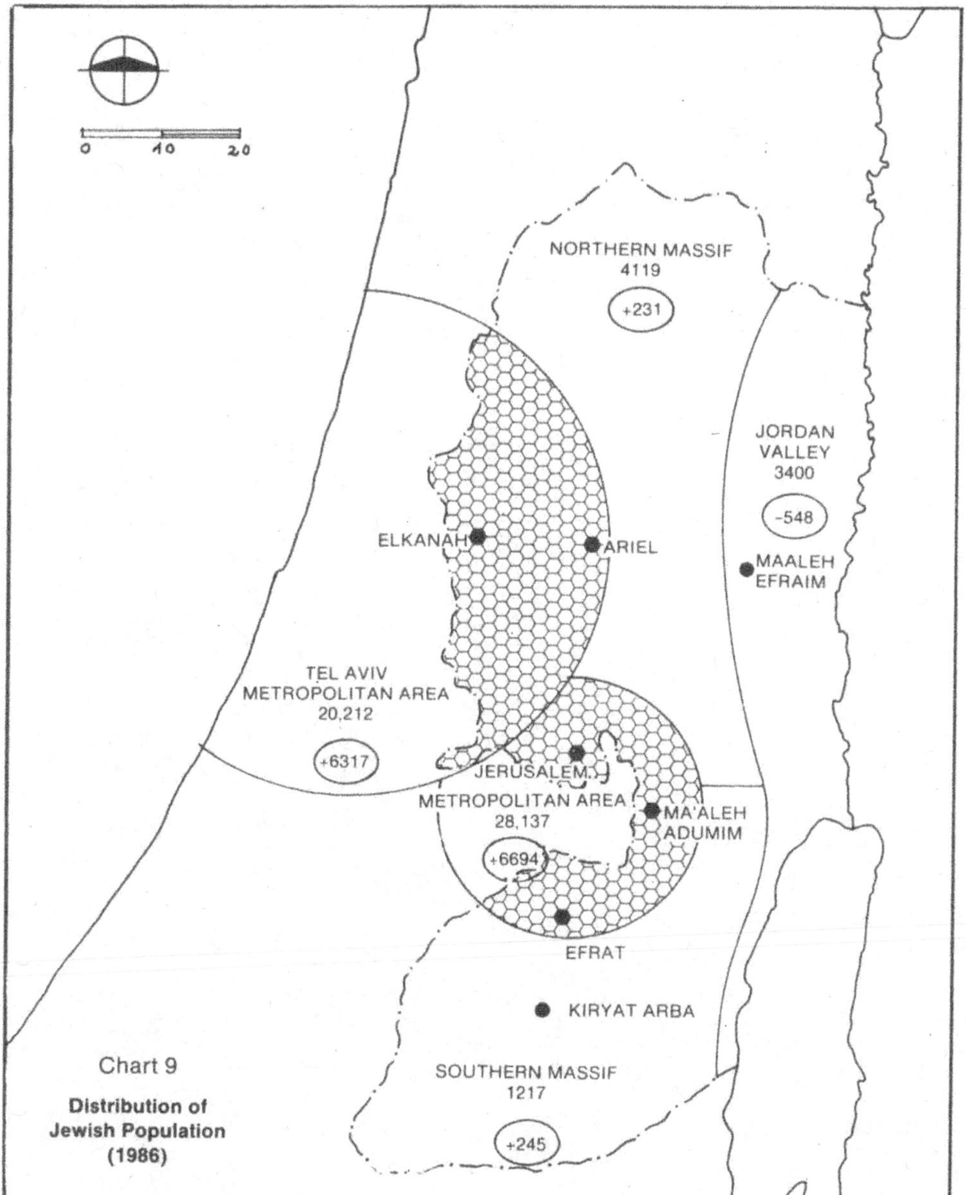

Chart 9

Distribution of Jewish Population (1986)

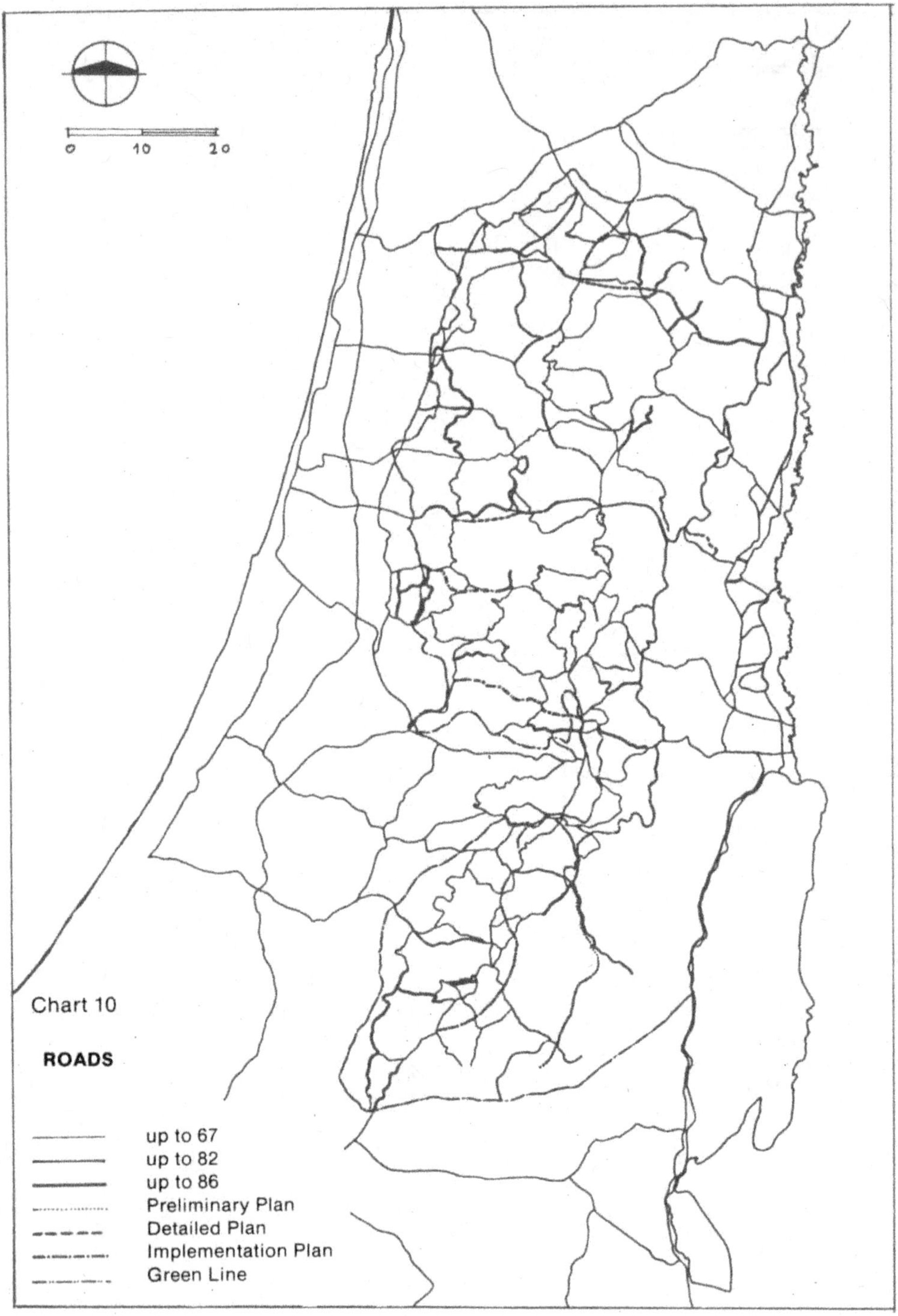
0 10 20
Chart 10
ROADS
up to 67
up to 82
up to 86
Preliminary Plan
Detailed Plan
Implementation Plan
Green Line